# Spies
# in the
# Sky

JOHN W.R. TAYLOR
DAVID MONDEY

# Spies
# in the
# Sky

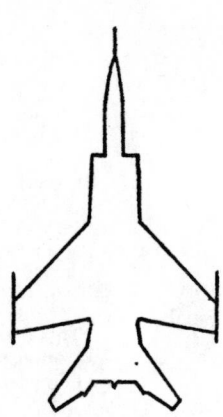

CHARLES SCRIBNER'S SONS
NEW YORK

A–12.72 (I)


Printed in Great Britain
Library of Congress Catalog Card Number 72–5709
SBN 684–13162–5 (Trade Cloth)

# Contents

| | | |
|---|---|---|
| *Introduction* | | 7 |
| 1 | The Elusive Foxbat | 11 |
| 2 | The New-Born Babe | 17 |
| 3 | Cloak and Dagger | 28 |
| 4 | How to Win the War | 38 |
| 5 | The Start of ECM | 45 |
| 6 | Open Skies | 53 |
| 7 | U–2 Story | 63 |
| 8 | On the Brink of World War III | 72 |
| 9 | Vietnam, and the Quiet Ones | 80 |
| 10 | ECM, AEW and ASW | 88 |
| 11 | Blackbirds and Peewits | 102 |
| 12 | Reconnaissance in the 'Seventies | 111 |
| *Index* | | 124 |

# Introduction

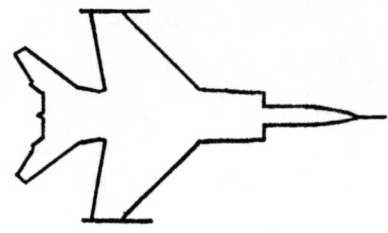

One of the most disturbing, almost frightening books written in our language is *Nineteen Eighty-Four*, the elaborate satire on modern politics by the late George Orwell. In prophesying the gradual degradation of personal liberty, he invented the all-seeing, all-knowing 'Big Brother'— a soulless, electronically-projected being dedicated to ensuring that all people conformed to the kind of lives considered best for them.

Today, less than a quarter of a century after *Nineteen Eighty-Four* was first published, 'Big Brother' is no longer fiction. We don't see him; most of us are unaware of his existence as he looks over our shoulder, watching for the slightest sign of anyone transgressing the rules. We might even ask "Whose rules? What rules?" The answer depends on whether this particular 'Big Brother' began life at Plesetsk or Tyuratam in the Soviet Union, or at Cape Kennedy or Point Arguello in the USA.

Orwell was right in giving electronic eyes to his political overseer. The counterparts of the 'seventies are satellites, sometimes twice as long as a motor coach. Packed full of television, cameras, infra-red eyes and electronic ears, they search out new rocket sites and military activities on the ground, a hundred miles below, while listening and learning about the types of radio and radar equipment which hold the key to the defensive capability of the 'other side'.

These sophisticated spies in the sky are more to be admired than feared. Before they attained their present standards of efficiency, aircraft packed with similar equipment had already uncovered a missile build-up in Cuba and supplied information which, backed up by a threat of thermonuclear striking power, persuaded the owners of the missiles to withdraw them. The world breathed easier for a time. Yet, only two years earlier, one of the 'spy-planes' itself had provoked a breakdown in East-West relations when it was shot down in a place where it had no legal right to be.

Our world must learn to live with these aerial 'Big Brothers', whether or not we like them. The Russians have demonstrated repeatedly that they could destroy American reconnaissance satellites whenever they wished. America may have possessed a similar capability since the mid-sixties. Neither side takes action, which would be entirely in accord with international law, because it cannot afford retaliatory measures against its own eyes and ears in the sky.

7

Thus, an uneasy peace is possible because any move towards major war, made by any nation on earth, would be known within hours in Washington and Moscow. On the basis of such knowledge, fingers would poise over buttons that could signal Armageddon. Peace through fear must always be preferable to a war precipitated by a less bearable fear of the unknown.

August 1972                                          John W. R. Taylor / David Mondey

# Spies
# in the
# Sky

# 1 The Elusive Foxbat

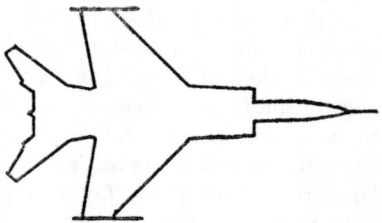

March 10th 1972, was a day of relative peace in the Middle East. Arab and Israeli soldiers watched each other suspiciously over the barrels of loaded guns along opposing banks of the Suez Canal. Periodically during the preceding weeks, President Sadat had hinted at the imminence of war to liberate enemy-occupied territories. For their part, the 'enemy' in Israel had become tired occasionally of Palestinian Arab tactics, and made swift, deadly raids across the border into Lebanon to destroy what they believed to be guerrilla bases.

Such a state of peace breeds tension scarcely less than that of open war. It could be sensed at every moment of every day at Cairo West. Nearly five years had gone by since the morning in June 1967 when Israeli jets crossed the Egyptian frontiers in wave after wave, to eliminate the air force of the United Arab Republic at nineteen airfields. Never had there been a more convincing demonstration of the effectiveness of air power, used imaginatively.

Israeli pilots knew every detail of the targets they attacked. They flew at least six sorties each on that first day, striking first at a time when they knew the Egyptians would have relaxed their vigil. They swept in low from the desert, or in a curving path over the Mediterranean, and used new weapons like the 'concrete dibber' bomb that grounded the opposition by chewing holes in vital runways.

Now the Egyptian air force was restored, stronger than ever in numbers and quality of aircraft. Clearly the Israelis would never get away with a repetition of that devastating pre-emptive strike of the 1967 Six-day War; but such knowledge offers little consolation. With an enemy as clever and resourceful as Israel, it is useless to practise methods of countering the last attack; it is the *next*, very different war that matters.

That is why the red, white and black, green-starred roundels of Egypt were less in evidence than the red stars of the Soviet Union on aircraft at Cairo West, until the Soviet forces were ordered out of Egypt in the summer of 1972. A war can be fought effectively, or prevented, only by knowing in advance of enemy preparations and intentions. The key to such knowledge, for nearly two centuries, has been aerial reconnaissance.

*11*

At Cairo West a pilot ambled slowly towards his aircraft. Let us call him Alexei Khrunov, although that is not his real name. Like 16,000 other Russians then in Egypt, his task was not to fight the Israelis but to help prevent another débâcle, by keeping a wary eye on every military movement by the 'other side'. That brief was not directed entirely at Middle Eastern political enemies. The big Tupolev Tu–16 bombers that flew out daily from Cairo West, far over the Mediterranean, were more concerned with watching the American Sixth Fleet than Egypt's troublesome neighbour; but Alexei is a fighter pilot, and was limited to closer targets.

He sweated inside his claustrophobic pressure-suit as he walked under the blazing sun towards his aircraft. The discomfort would soon pass. He knew that within minutes he would be climbing steeply to a height at which his blood would boil without the suit's constriction, although the temperature outside his cockpit would be 75 degrees below zero Centigrade.

It is usual for such a man to love the aircraft he flies. Even in an electronic age, his are the eyes, ears, brain and hands that, joined to its metallic power, can outpace the sun or destroy an enemy that is never seen, at night or in bad weather. In Alexei's case, he has the satisfaction of knowing also that his is the fastest combat aircraft in service with any air force in the world.

One of the last great designs by Artem Mikoyan, the MiG–23 first hit the headlines with a series of record-breaking flights in the mid-sixties. By October 1967 it had proved its ability to climb to a height of nearly 100,000ft (30,000m) carrying a two-ton load, and to fly round a circular course at speeds of up to 1,852mph (2,981km/h). Western engineers did not need to wield their slide-rules for long before deciding that this was the first of an entirely new and formidable breed of Soviet combat aircraft.

Earlier MiGs had relied for their performance on small size and light weight. In Korea in the early 'fifties the original MiG–15 jet-fighter, with an engine based on the Rolls-Royce Nene, had compared well with America's F–86 Sabre. It excelled in rate of climb, tightness of turn and service ceiling, and was faster than the Sabre above 35,000ft (10,660m). The fact that Russia still had much to learn was indicated only by a few unpleasant little tricks that detracted from its efficiency as a weapon platform.

The MiG–15 sometimes flicked over into a snap roll and uncontrollable spin if its pilot tried to pull too tight a turn to escape a pursuing Sabre. It lacked stability at really high speeds and had few of the advanced items of equipment, such as a radar gunsight, that were taken for granted in the US Air Force.

Performance and handling qualities were improved on the MiG–17. The MiG–19 brought transition to supersonic speed in level flight; by this time, too, air-to-air missiles supplemented the original heavy-calibre guns, and the night-fighter versions were fitted with radar to track down their quarry.

The MiG–21 brought a huge stride forward. Despite its tiny size, with a wing span of only 23ft 5½in (7.15m), it could fly at twice the speed of sound and had the delightful handling qualities of a real 'pilot's aeroplane'. Any reasonably competent pilot could fly it, and MiG–21s have been built in thousands, for some twenty air forces. The original version was short on fuel, radar and weapons; but each new version has brought improvements, and the latest MiG–21MFs which shared Cairo West with the –23s and Tu–16s are potent combat aircraft for a variety of roles. Even so, the –23 is in a class apart.

When foreign air attachés first glimpsed it at the 1967 Soviet Aviation Day display at Domodedovo Airport, Moscow, their reports told of a big, twin-engined, twin-finned aircraft that might well outfly anything in the West. The record flights that year indicated that it could cruise at three times the speed of sound. With a span of around 40ft (12.2m) and two engines giving a total of 48,500lb (22,000kg) of thrust, it clearly departed from the familiar minimum-size, minimum-weight MiG formula. Under-wing weapon attachments conformed with the 1967 commentator's remark that it was designed as a high-altitude interceptor, as did the search radar in its nose; but subsequent study of photographs revealed weapon bays forward of each main wheel bay in the big engine air-intake ducts.

Code-naming it 'Foxbat', NATO began to study every new picture or report of the MiG–23 with particular care. The results remained secret, and the public heard little of the new aircraft between 1967 and 1971. Then, in the Spring of that year, the aircraft equipping Alexei's unit were airlifted to Egypt in huge An–22 turboprop freighters.

It was a significant move. For years, Egypt had suffered from a lack of aircraft able to fly over Israel or Israeli military installations in occupied territories. Any attempt to make a quick, unexpected reconnaissance met with a swift reaction from vigilant, well-trained pilots, flying aircraft like the American-built Phantom, armed with air-to-air homing missiles.

Somebody reported, many years ago, that when the British Hawker Aircraft company abandoned further work on its P.1121 fighter, Egypt offered to pay £14 million for the prototype, which was then half-completed, and a second aircraft of the same type. Colonel Nasser realised that these aircraft, able to fly at Mach 2.5 (two-and-a-half times the speed of sound), would be able to overfly Israel at will, without fear of interception. But such a sale was clearly out of the question in the years following the 1956 Suez campaign.

In 1971, the gap was filled by the MiG–23. Long known to have a performance adequate for such reconnaissance missions, its capability was first demonstrated on October 10th that year. Taking off from Cairo West, two of Alexei's colleagues had flown out over the Mediterranean and approached the Israeli coast near Acre, in the far North, at great speed and height. Staying some 18 miles (29km) out to sea, they had then followed the entire coastline of Israel and Sinai on their way home. Knowing the capability of modern reconnaissance devices, even in a 'side-looking' mode, this was a clear warning to Israel that its defences could be penetrated and exposed to 'enemy' cameras and electronic sensors whenever the other side wished.

In fact, with a customary strict observance of legality, the Soviet pilots made no attempt to overfly Israel itself. The coastal flight had been in the nature of a warning; practical missions were to be limited to an aerial observation of Israel's military positions in the Sinai Peninsula, taken from Egypt in 1967.

On November 6th 1971, two MiG–23s approached Sinai rather cautiously from the sea and raced over the North-Western corner of the occupied region before crossing the Gulf of Suez to the relative safety of Egypt. Israel protested to United Nations cease-fire officials; but such complaints achieve little in a world that hesitates even to turn military forces out of occupied territories as long as their aggression does not threaten the major balance of East-West power.

For Alexei's unit, the November sorties had confirmed that the Israeli Air Force was unable to intercept MiG–23s, even with aircraft as good as the Phantom. So Alexei and another pilot were to take advantage of this knowledge by probing the defences along almost the entire length of Sinai.

As he strapped himself into the MiG's cockpit and prepared for take-off, he saw a flight of MiG–21s taxi out and climb away from the airfield, with pairs of K–13 homing air-to-air missiles projecting viciously from their underwing rails. Although far slower than his –23 at height, these lightly-loaded fighters were more agile at lower altitudes. Consequently, they were always 'scrambled' before a –23 take-off, to provide protection from Israeli intruders until the bigger machine had climbed to a safer height.

Through the headphones built into his spaceman-like helmet, Alexei received word that the –21s were in position to cover his take-off. Doubtless, their movements had been detected by the Israelis, who might guess what was to follow. So, with no time to waste, Alexei slammed open the throttles of his two turbojets, and streaked down Cairo West's runway into the air.

Within a minute the MiG–21s were far below, as he set course for the cease-fire line along the Suez Canal, still climbing like a rocket. To his left he could see the second –23, paralleling his every move.

Sinai is some 250 miles (400km) long from North to South. From a height of 80,000ft (24,400m), it was laid out like a page from a school atlas—so remote and lacking in detail that the possibility of its being peopled with armies of men, equipped with tanks, aircraft, missiles, guns and every form of modern military store, seemed difficult to believe. Yet Alexei knew that his life would be worth little if he dived to low altitude for a closer look.

As the MiGs sped at Mach 2.5 on a Southeasterly course, from about 9½ miles (15km) North of Ismailia towards the Israel stronghold of Sharm el Sheikh at the tip of the peninsula, cameras and electronic gear worked automatically to reveal details that were invisible and inaudible to the pilots. Very little of what was happening below would escape these photographic and scientific sensors.

Warning messages from ground control in Egypt told Alexei that Phantoms had taken off to hunt him. They got near enough to produce tiny blips on the warning radar screen on his instrument panel, but not close enough to loose their missiles. What chance did they really have when the entire overflight—the first to cross the cease-fire line, and probably unexpected—lasted a mere ten minutes?

Still keeping close company, the two MiGs banked steeply on to a Westerly course that took them over the Gulf of Suez, and were soon beginning their let-down towards their base. It had all been very quick, very easy, and very safe; yet hundreds of pilots had died in two World Wars in efforts to bring back a fraction of the information that their reconnaissance equipment would reveal to skilled interpreters. Alexei himself seemed to have played such a small part in the whole business that he felt almost a fraud—a pilot who could simply enjoy flying, in complete security, through skies in which other men, in lesser aircraft, might die through simply crossing an unmarked line between 'them' and 'us'.

'They', in this case, had nothing like the MiG–23 and could not perform similar missions to uncover Egyptian and Soviet installations to the West of Suez. The nagging question, to which there was no answer, was whether this mattered to the Israelis.

At the time of the 1967 Six-day War, there had been persistent suggestions that Israel knew just when, where and how to strike because her government had access to information gathered by American reconnaissance satellites. Whether or not this was true, it was indisputable that such information was, and is, available to the US services and to those of its allies and friends who might seem to need the facts for their wellbeing. With the Soviet Union providing such open military aid to the Arabs, it is unrealistic to believe that America would fail to warn Israel of any military build-up that might precede an Arab offensive.

This really cut Alexei down to size, because it seemed that a glorified 'tin dustbin', filled with electronic gadgetry and cameras, could do just as good a job as a highly trained pilot in the world's fastest combat aeroplane.

How far this is true at the present time we can only guess. One fact we do know is that in July 1970 a Lockheed-built reconnaissance satellite was launched from Vandenberg Air Force Base, California, and put into an orbit that would enable it to survey areas of the Middle East subject to the subsequent Arab-Israeli cease-fire agreement. This, a mere thirteen years after the first 184.3lb (83.6kg) Sputnik bleeped its way round the Earth for three months.

Another indication of the decreasing need for men in the air, or above it, was America's abandonment of plans to put a manned orbiting laboratory (MOL) into orbit above the Earth, carrying a USAF crew. Aside from scientific research, the MOL was envisaged in 1965–68 as a long-endurance reconnaissance vehicle in which two men could live and work in a 'shirt-sleeve' environment for periods of up to thirty days. The results obtained by the latest US military satellites are said to be so satisfactory that they justify entirely the decision to scrap the MOL.

However, for the first 170 years of aerial reconnaissance there was no substitute for a man and his eyes, as we shall see in the next chapter.

# 2 The New-Born Babe

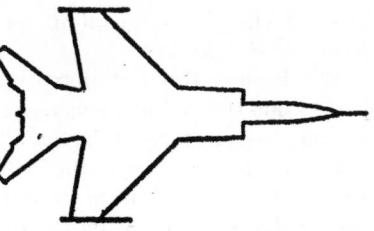

Flying has always suffered from the sceptics. From the dawn of civilisation, whenever anyone broached the subject of human flight he risked the rebuff that: 'If God had meant men to fly, He would have given them wings.'

Even when the pioneer balloon-makers of the 18th century proved that wings were not essential as a means of getting airborne, the sceptics remained unimpressed.

Benjamin Franklin, the great American scientist-statesman, told of an encounter he had with such a person during the first, pilotless demonstration of a hydrogen balloon on August 27th 1783. As Professor Charles' silken 'flying globe' was released, and disappeared into low rain-filled clouds, someone turned to Franklin with the remark: "Interesting. But what use is it?" Sharply, the ageing American growled back: "Of what use is a new-born baby?"

Seeing far beyond the capabilities of that 13ft (4m) sphere, he wrote to fellow-scientists in Philadelphia, London and Vienna, stressing its military potential. He did not live long enough to see his predictions come true; but they did—within a decade!

Knowledge of an enemy's dispositions and movements had always been a key to success in war. Spies and infiltrators gathered precious scraps of intelligence at the risk of their lives; cavalry were trained for quick forays in battle areas to locate and report at high speed the whereabouts of the opposition. The objective, always, was to find out what was happening on the other side of the hill on land, or over the horizon at sea.

Even in its primitive form, the balloon offered this capability. As early as 1784 an anonymous gentleman in France published a treatise entitled *L'Art de la Guerre changé par l'usage de Machines Aérostatiques*. It was premature to suggest that the balloons of that time might change the whole art of war; but in the early 1790s a distinguished chemist named Guyton de Morveau put forward such a strong case for using captive balloons for reconnaissance that Captain J. M. J. Coutelle was instructed to carry out experiments at Meudon in April 1794.

The results were sufficiently encouraging to prompt the formation of a balloon division; and Coutelle was despatched, with balloon, to test the 'eyes in the sky' concept under fire, as a member of General Jourdan's Army of the Moselle.

The French Revolutionary Wars had reached a crucial stage. Jourdan had 73,000 troops entrenched in a 20mile (32km) semi-circle of strongpoints around the captured town of Charleroi. Such a disposition stretched his army to the limit; but the Allied commander-in-chief, Prince Josias of Saxe-Coburg, divided his numerically-inferior force to an even-greater degree. He drew up a plan under which his army attacked the French in three columns. In doing so he worked out the operation so minutely that there was no possibility of changes to remedy the situation if things began to go wrong.

How great a part Captain Coutelle played in this Battle of Fleurus, on June 26th 1794, is debatable. Some detailed accounts fail to mention his name; but J. E. Hodgson's famous *History of Aeronautics*, published in 1924, gives great credit to this first military airman.

As Coutelle clambered into the basket of his balloon and began to rise into the air above the heads of Jourdan's soldiers on that June day, he must have seen a frightening sight. Camouflage was a century away in the future and, never having been subjected to aerial observation, the Allied troops in their bright, handsome uniforms would have made little attempt to conceal themselves as they flooded in towards the French positions.

How intrigued Coutelle must have been as he watched the whole course of the battle unfolding beneath his balloon, like figures moving over a huge, deadly chess-board. Too high to see the horrible detail of how men died, and beyond the reach of the enemy, he stayed aloft for several hours. According to Hodgson: "The information which he signalled to Jourdan proved to be a material factor in the far-reaching victory which the French forces gained over the Allies, and the achievement was repeated in the subsequent battle on the Ourthe, near Liège, when the French defeated the Austrians."

Support for this estimate of the worth of Coutelle's observation flights is provided by an official French decision to expand the 'Company of Aérostiers' and add a new cylindrical balloon to its strength; but enthusiasm was short-lived. After a few more successful operational ascents in Europe, Coutelle was sent to Egypt by Napoleon in 1798. Before the Aérostiers could unload their equipment in Abukir bay, near Alexandria, a British fleet under Rear Admiral Sir Horatio Nelson arrived on the scene. The ensuing Battle of the Nile, on August 1st, turned the tide of what had seemed to be an irresistible wave of conquest by France. Napoleon was to remain a thorn in the flesh of his enemies for another seventeen years; the Aérostiers, with little to show for their expedition across the Mediterranean, survived only until 1799.

This was by no means the end of the observation balloon. It served in America in 1861, during the Civil War, and became a standard item of equipment with British expeditionary forces in Africa later in the century. New lease of life followed its elongation into the sausage-shaped *Drachen*, or kite-balloon, by von Parseval and von Sigsfeld in Germany, in 1897; and balloons of this type were used by both sides down the length of the Western Front in France in the World War of 1914–18. But by then aerial reconnaissance was no longer restricted by the length of a tethering cable.

A new and far more efficient kind of reconnaissance aircraft had been born a few feet above the sands of Kill Devil Hills, near Kitty Hawk, North Carolina, just after 10.30 on the morning of December 17th 1903. In perfecting the first aeroplane able to make a powered, controlled and sustained flight, the Wright brothers had pointed the way to a vehicle that could search out the enemy in a wide combat area and follow his every movement, many miles from the nearest 'friendly' territory.

Recalling their early ambitions to fly, and looking back on the devastation of war, Orville Wright commented in 1918: "What a dream it was. What a nightmare it has become." Yet the Wrights never had any illusions about the machine they created. As early as June 15th 1907, Orville had written to the US War Department: "We believe that the principal use of a flyer at present is for military purposes". Within four years that particular dream materialised, in North Africa.

The first recorded use of an aeroplane in war took place on October 23rd 1911. Significantly, it was a reconnaissance sortie.

Italy and Turkey were fighting for possession of Tripolitania and Cyrenaica; and the Italian ground forces were supported by a handful of frail and primitive aeroplanes. Determined to prove their worth in a climate that was totally unsuited to machines of wood and fabric, with engines of feeble power, the pilots planned a series of flights that displayed great imagination and courage.

Captain Piazza was first to take off, in a monoplane similar to that in which Louis Blériot had crossed the English Channel two years earlier. Blériot would have ended up in the sea if a providential shower of rain had not cooled his overheating engine at the opportune moment. Captain Piazza must have thought of this as he ascended into the much warmer skies over Africa; but he remained airborne for an hour and was able to report valuable details of what he had seen on the ground between Tripoli and Azizia.

Nine days later this tiny Italian air detachment made the first-ever bombing raid. It then switched to what we regard as the modern science of psychological warfare, by showering the local Arabs with propaganda leaflets rather than more bombs, inviting them to change sides.

Within eight years of its birth, the aeroplane had learned to hunt and to kill, long before it showed any signs of commercial usefulness. And already the man at the controls was thinking in terms of weapons and equipment that would increase its military effectiveness.

Realising that the pilot had his hands full when flying and navigating his aircraft, without having to draw maps and make notes during reconnaissance sorties, Captain Piazza again made history on February 24th and 25th 1912, when he photographed Turkish positions from the air. On

April 19th Commandant Sulsi carried the idea an important stage further by taking a ciné-film of an enemy encampment from the military airship P.3.

This was made possible by the much greater lifting capacity and roominess of the airships of that time, by comparison with contemporary aeroplanes. Germany, too, had appreciated their capability, and her Zeppelin airships were in many respects the most formidable military aircraft of the early period of World War I. They are remembered usually for the bombing raids they made on London and other targets in Britain. In fact, the primary duty of the German Naval Airship Division was reconnaissance over the North Sea, and they performed it superbly. Whatever successes the German Navy achieved were due in large measure to the ceaseless watch that the Zeppelins kept on Allied shipping movements, and each airship was reckoned to be worth five or six cruisers for this reason alone.

Eventually, the Zeppelins were made obsolete by the rapid progress of the military aeroplane. Even at their ceiling of 12,000 to 16,000ft (3,500–5,000m) the hydrogen-filled giants were terribly vulnerable to aircraft firing incendiary ammunition and to phosphor shells from anti-aircraft guns. What is often overlooked is that the combat aircraft evolved so rapidly in 1915–16 mainly because it became essential to hamper the 'other side's' aerial reconnaissance activities.

For a time, the newly created air forces of most countries seemed to ignore the pioneering Italian operations in North Africa in 1911–12. Typically, the British Royal Flying Corps was regarded as a potential form of airborne light cavalry for scouting when it came into existence on May 13th 1912; and when military trials were held on Salisbury Plain three months later, to find the best aircraft for the new service, the emphasis was on reconnaissance capability.

The trials proved a complete flop. Under the impractical system of 'scoring' that had been devised, the winner was a massive bamboo-and-wire biplane built by the flamboyant 'Colonel' S. F. Cody. Far superior was the B.E.2 biplane, flown to Salisbury Plain by its designer, Geoffrey de Havilland; but it was not allowed to compete in the contests because it was a product of the state-run Royal Aircraft Factory at Farnborough.

In the event, only two Cody biplanes were ordered for the RFC, whereas the B.E.2 entered massive production as its standard equipment. Paradoxically, the very qualities which made it so outstanding were responsible for its downfall.

Research at Farnborough in those early years was aimed primarily at producing an aeroplane so inherently stable that it could be left to fly itself while the pilot devoted his eyes, thoughts and hands to reconnaissance duties. By 1914, the developed B.E.2c version of Geoffrey de Havilland's basic design came close to that ideal.

Well over a thousand B.E.2s of various kinds were built for the RFC. One of them, flown by Captain (later Air Chief Marshal Sir) Philip Joubert de la Ferté, made the first reconnaissance flight over enemy territory in World War I, on August 19th 1914, in company with a Blériot XI monoplane flown by Lt Gilbert Mapplebeck. It was hardly successful, as Joubert recalled later in his autobiography.*

"Flying for the first time on 1/1,000,000 maps, both of us went adrift. Gilbert lost himself on the way back to Maubeuge, and I spent most of the day flying round parts of Belgium to which I had not been instructed to go. After getting lost over the coal-mining area of Mons I finally decided to land at a large town where the houses still seemed to be flying the Belgian flag. This was Tournai, where my aircraft was refuelled and I was given lunch by the Commandant of the place. From there I took off again, lost myself once more and, running out of fuel, landed near Courtrai. Here my reception was not at all friendly. It had not occurred to the War Office to provide us with identification papers and a good many of us were to experience difficulty owing to this lack of forethought. I was on my way to prison in Courtrai when I was saved by the intervention of a little Belfast linen manufacturer. He was in the crowd around the aircraft and, hearing me swear very heartily, rushed forward, shouting: 'Och, shure and he's an Englishman,' and taking from his pocket a small Union Jack, hung it on the aircraft. Immediately, the atmosphere changed. My aircraft was refuelled and I was given directions as to how to reach Waterloo, over which I finally did my reconnaissance and, tired but thankful, regained Maubeuge—having long ago been given up as dead. Both reconnaissances were negative, but at least they showed that the defence of Liège had held up the German advance."

Further setbacks followed that inauspicious beginning. No 6 Squadron was prepared for foreign service at such haste that its observers received only the barest training. In France they mistook long patches of tar on macadamized roads for troops on the march; shadows cast by tombstones in a cemetery were interpreted as military bivouacs. In consequence, field commanders began to distrust reports received from the four squadrons of assorted aircraft despatched to the Western Front by the RFC.

Their scepticism soon underwent a dramatic change. During the retreat from Mons, the RFC helped the British army to escape German enveloping movements that might otherwise have trapped and eliminated it. The commander of the British Expeditionary Force, Field-Marshal Sir John French, commented in his first despatch, on September 7th 1914: "I wish particularly to bring to your Lordship's notice the admirable work done by the Royal Flying Corps. Their skill, energy and perseverance have been beyond all praise. They have furnished me with the most complete and accurate information, which has been of incalculable value in the conduct of operations."

Unfortunately, wars are not won by retreats, however successful, and the situation was now desperate. On the Marne, the armies under General Joffre formed a last-ditch defence between the victorious Germans and

* *The Fated Sky* (Hutchinson, 1952).

Paris, a mere month after the declaration of war. On September 6th, just before the crucial battle began, Sir John French redeployed his small air component. Three aircraft of No 5 Squadron were despatched to provide direct tactical reconnaissance for the British First Army Corps under Sir Douglas Haig: three aircraft of No 3 Squadron were allocated to General Sir Horace Smith-Dorrien's Second Army Corps for similar duties. Thus began the decentralisation of the RFC, whereby certain units, which came to be called corps squadrons, were attached to the corps commands—a practice adopted from the beginning by the German air service. It worked well.

By September 9th the Battle of the Marne was over. Paris was saved and an invading Prussian army had been driven back for the first time in more than a hundred years. In a message to Sir John French, Joffre said: "Please express most particularly my thanks for the services rendered to us every day by the English Flying Corps. The precision, exactitude, and regularity of the news brought in by them are evidence of their perfect organisation and also of the perfect training of pilots and observers."

Aerial reconnaissance was in business; but only one battle had been won and the war was hardly started. Crude techniques needed refining, and the problems multiplied as fast as the successes.

Winter weather caused a major setback on December 28th when a violent storm wrecked thirty aircraft of the small RFC force in France, sixteen of them beyond repair. Even more disturbing, the enemy was quick to react to the threat of unrestricted observation of his dispositions and movements, and sought every means of interfering with the reconnaissance operations.

The aerial dogfights of World War I are pictured romantically as tourneys between airborne counterparts of mediaeval knights in shining armour. The 'Red Barons', McCuddens and Guynemers of 1914–18 may have engaged in many fighter-to-fighter combats, but this was not their primary role.

Air fighting first became important as a means of preventing enemy reconnaissance. This became apparent as early as July 1915 when the Germans began operating Fokker monoplanes, the world's first true fighter aircraft with a synchronised forward-firing machine-gun. Main targets for the Fokkers were the British B.E.2c reconnaissance aircraft. Their inherent stability made them almost incapable of aerobatics, so that they were easily outmanoeuvred by the agile Fokkers. Nor could they defend themselves. The observer, in the front cockpit, had a gun but was so hedged in by wings, struts and wires that he seldom had a clear field of fire as the enemy attacked. During the nine months of what became known as 'the Fokker scourge', the B.E.2c is said to have been responsible for more casualties in a given period than any other RFC type.

Until the RFC had fighters of its own, as good as the Fokkers, it had to adopt desperate measures. Its pilots had to learn to fly in formation, in order to benefit from mutual defence and a greater concentration of their inadequate fire-power. The lengths to which this was carried can be gauged by a planned reconnaissance mission over Belgian railway lines on February 7th 1916, when a single B.E.2c was allocated an escort of three other B.E.2cs, four F.E.s, a Bristol Scout and four R.Es.

The scourge ended only when new British and French fighters were put into service to fight off the Fokkers. The original duties of the fighter were, therefore, to protect friendly reconnaissance aircraft, destroy enemy reconnaissance aircraft and, in so doing, engage enemy fighters in combat. Bombers had as their main original objective the destruction of bases from which enemy aircraft operated—with particular emphasis on the Zeppelins and aeroplanes used for reconnaissance. Fighters then added to their responsibilities the protection or destruction of bombers; while the bombers sprouted guns for their own defence. So the entire range of military types grew out of what began as a simple requirement for manned aerial cavalry.

As World War I dragged on, year after weary year, reconnaissance itself grew in scope and efficiency. What it entailed was told superbly by H. A. Jones in Volume II of the official history of the part played by the RFC and RAF in World War I:*

"Air reconnaissance was now in the nature of a routine insurance against surprise. Broadly speaking, it settled to two kinds—tactical and strategical. Tactical reconnaissance may be said to be confined to the immediate battle area to locate and examine trenches, gun emplacements, reserves, and railheads, chiefly to satisfy the corps or divisional commanders who wish to know what there is on their immediate front, as well as the changes that take place from day to day, so that they may make their local dispositions to the best purpose. Strategical reconnaissance, which begins where tactical leaves off, helps the commander of an army to know his opponent's mind, and to deduce his plan of campaign.

"Before the infantry came to learn in France something of the peculiarities of air observation, they sometimes complained that German airmen were up at dawn to search for our troops, whereas the Flying Corps were much later astir and were most active in the evening; but the blame is with the sun which rises in the east. In the early morning the German airmen were often in the best position to see, whereas the visibility into the sun, always limited, might be too poor for any observation of value to the British airmen.

"A word or two on what the airman can see will help to illustrate the value of reconnaissance. Digging cannot effectively be concealed. Tracks show up clearly: a track which might be passed over on the ground and not noticed, will be plain thousands of feet up. One man walking along a road may be clearly visible, but men walking across country, unless they are in close formation, can hardly be seen above three thousand feet. There are some who think that if they look up from the ground their white faces will be visible, but this is only true if the face of the observer be distinguishable also as he looks over the side of his aeroplane. Objects or men concealed in

* *The War in the Air* (by permission of The Clarendon Press, Oxford).

the shadow cast by some other object are most difficult to detect. On the other hand, moving objects, on a sunny day, will often be first revealed by their moving shadows. Men may remain unseen in a wood or in a village if they do not reveal themselves by movement, by smoke from their fires, or, for instance, by firing at the aeroplane.

"One of the most tell-tale things which an observer may see, in stationary warfare, is rolling-stock at the rail-heads behind the enemy front. Important movements cannot be made without concentrations of road or rail transport, and the airmen, by keeping the enemy's rail and military centres under regular observation, especially at daybreak and sundown, may surprise movements which anticipate the night or which have been over-taken by the dawn. . . . The army intelligence staff working on the reports brought in throughout the day, examining, comparing, assessing, gradually piece together the story of the enemy; the effect of their deductions appears in the orders which the army commander issues to his troops.

"Reconnaissance work is not spectacular. A flying officer has compared it with the routine of going to the office daily, the aeroplane being sub-stituted for the suburban train. The officer does his daily job and goes home; the board sit in debate over the profit and loss account."

What would that particular flying officer feel about modern recon-naissance? As will be seen later in this book, men concealed on the ground still reveal themselves, fatally, by opening fire on the 'spy-planes' overhead; but concealment is becoming more and more difficult in an age when aircraft carry 'sniffers' to smell out men and machines on the ground and infra-red devices which can pick up the heat of human bodies in the dark or among the foliage of dense forest. On the other hand, suburban commuters do not have to endure an early morning train ride punctuated by deadly cannon-fire, guided missiles and other forms of unpleasantness. So the 1914–18 simile no longer carries full credence.

In 1915, a soldier walking cross-country was difficult to detect from even a height of 3,000ft (900m). Today, huge robot satellites orbit the Earth, carrying cameras that can identify man-size detail from a height of more than 100 miles (160km). The first stage of that fantastic evolution took place in September 1914, when pilots of No 3 Squadron, RFC, took photo-graphs of enemy trenches during the battle of the Aisne. They were indis-tinct, and the army staff showed little enthusiasm.

The French were achieving far better results. So, after studying the equipment and organisation of the photographic reconnaissance (PR) units of their allies, the RFC formed an experimental section whose task was to report on how British PR should be organised, and the best type of camera that it could use to ensure equally valuable service to the army. The section consisted of Lt J. T. C. Moore-Brabazon (later Lord Brabazon of Tara), Lt C. D. M. Campbell, Flt Sgt F. C. V. Laws (now one of the great names in commercial air survey) and 2nd Air Mechanic W. D. Corse. These men were soon busy on the design of a new camera, and from their work sprang the whole sophisticated science of military PR.

Known as the 'A' camera, their pioneer design was produced in co-operation with the Thornton-Pickard Manufacturing Company and made use of the Mackenzie-Wishart 5 × 4inch (13 × 10cm) slide and envelope. H. A. Jones recorded in *The War in the Air* that: 'It took the form of a conical box, built to withstand rough usage, with the lens in a recessed front at a fixed distance from the plate. The observer gripped the camera through straps or brass handles as he leaned over the side of the aeroplane to take his photographs. The chief objection to the camera was that the first exposure called for eleven distinct operations, and each subsequent exposure ten. This was no small demand to make on an observer, already keyed to high tension, who had to lean from his cockpit into a gale of wind and fumble through thick gloves or with fingers numbed by cold.'

Gradually, techniques were improved. To ensure the acquisition of true vertical photographs for mapping, it was soon decided to fix the camera to the aircraft, which improved the lot of the observer. By mid-1915 a semi-automatic plate-changing mechanism had been produced on the 'C' camera.

Well before this, the reorganised PR units had proved their worth. As the first stage of its Spring offensive, Sir Douglas Haig's First Army set out to capture the village of Neuve Chapelle. Before it did so, Nos 2 and 3 Squadrons photographed the entire German trench system in front of the Army to a depth of 700 to 1,500 yards (640–1,370m). The entrenchments were traced carefully on skeleton maps of 1:8,000 scale, and details of the plan of attack were based on these maps.

Quoting H. A. Jones again: 'Orders for the artillery were drawn up after a study of the positions of the various defended points, as revealed by the air photographs. Furthermore, it was possible to deduce, from the direction of the communication trenches, what the main line of approach of the enemy would be. Some fifteen hundred copies of the map were issued to each of the army corps before the attack, so that, for the first time in its history, the British army went into action with a picture of the hidden intricacies of the enemy defences. After the first assault, bombing parties were able to make their way, without loss of time, to their separate objectives.'

So was set a pattern which was followed, with steadily-refined results, until the war's end. What had begun so inauspiciously was regarded by 1918 as being utterly vital. Countless sorties, on every day when flying was possible, kept up-to-date a huge photographic map of the entire Western Front, in thousands of sections. The extent of the effort this entailed is shown by the fact that 10,441 photographs were taken in a single week before the great German offensive on the Somme, in March 1918, to warn and aid the Allied troops who had to bear the brunt of the onslaught. Often, prints were in the hands of a corps commander within an hour of the exposure of the plates over enemy lines.

In the final stages of the war, more than 35 per cent of all the aeroplanes in service with the newly-formed RAF were classed as corps reconnaissance or two-seat reconnaissance-fighter aircraft. Mainstay of the force was the R.E.8, designed at the Royal Aircraft Factory to supersede the B.E.2c: over 2,000 were used on the Western Front alone, and the R.E.8 must have accumulated more flying hours than any other single type. Its main task was to observe and correct the fire of Allied guns—known as 'artillery spotting'—and in his standard reference work on *British Aeroplanes 1914–18*,* J. M. Bruce comments: "Those who flew in France during the years 1917 and 1918 are not likely to forget the seemingly ever-present R.E.8, flying its stolid, elliptical course, and trailing a wake of anti-aircraft shell-bursts behind it. That it did much good in this way is to the credit of the pilots and observers who flew it. The R.E.8 was given to them without choice of alternative: in it they did their duty."

That duty was made possible by the introduction of improved air-to-ground radio, in the same way that reconnaissance had progressed through the development of special cameras. Early wireless sets weighed about 75lb (34kg) and were so bulky that the two-seat aeroplanes in which they were installed could not carry an observer, the apparatus not only filling the observer's cockpit but overflowing into the pilot's compartment. By the Autumn of 1915, this problem was overcome by perfection of the Sterling set, weighing under 20lb (9kg) and leaving plenty of room for a crew of two.

Messages were transmitted to the gun crews by means of a specially-concocted 'clock code'. The observer in the aircraft and the man on the ground each had a celluloid disc with circles inserted at 10 to 500 yards radius, according to the scale of the map in use. The circles were lettered and the figures of a clock-face were printed outside them, with the XII–VI line orientated as true north–south. It was then simple to signal the position of any shell-burst as, say, C9 or B2, after placing the centre of the disc over the position of the intended target on the map. This gave the artillery all the information they needed to correct their aim quickly.

Inevitably, the Germans did everything possible to hamper the work of the R.E.8s, whether the latter were engaged on PR or artillery spotting. Sometimes they received a shock. On August 16th 1917, an R.E.8 of No 7 Squadron was set upon by two Albatros fighters while taking photographs during the battle of Langemarck. Its observer promptly shot down one of the enemy; the other decided to go home. Later that day, another aircraft from the same Squadron was attacked by eight Albatros'. One of the enemy was despatched with a single 60-round burst of fire from close range, after which that R.E.8 too was left to finish its work in peace.

More often, the reconnaissance pilots came off second-best in their duels with faster, more manoeuvrable and more numerous enemies. On April 13th 1917, for example, six R.E.8s of 59 Squadron were pounced upon by von Richthofen's fighters while undertaking an early-morning PR sortie. Four of the British aircraft were supposed to provide escort for the remaining

* Putnam, 1957.

two, which carried cameras. This was considered adequate, as at least three Allied fighter patrols were expected to be in the same area. In the event, the fighter pilots never caught sight of the R.E.8s, all of which were destroyed.

Such was the cost of proving the capability and indispensability of aerial reconnaissance.

# 3 Cloak and Dagger

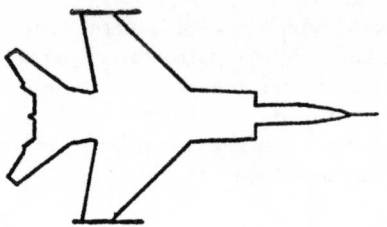

"Would you be prepared to undertake a secret mission for French and British intelligence sources?"

What would be your reaction to such an enquiry, however phrased and no matter how delicately the subject was approached? No doubt it would come as something of a shock, and unless you were an adventurous type the answer, most likely, would be in the negative.

Sidney Cotton's answer, when faced with a similar proposal, was an assured affirmative. It appealed to the prime interests of his life, so who could want more?

Born in 1894, Cotton was one of many Australians who came to Britain during World War I, determined to fight for the Allied cause. He lost little time in joining the Royal Naval Air Service and, with natural aptitude as a pilot, was soon posted to an operational air wing.

His fellow-pilots included such well-known characters as Spenser Grey and Reggie Marix, and it was while serving in France that he designed the Sidcot (*Sid*ney *Cot*ton) flying suit that, for many years, was considered an essential part of the well-dressed airman's flying kit.

Cotton's career in the RNAS was comparatively short-lived. Like many men of fertile brain, he was both eccentric and outspoken and it was not long before he crossed swords with the fiery Commodore Godfrey Paine. Unable to accept the latter officer's interpretation of a matter of discipline, Cotton resigned his commission and went home to Australia.

Several years of ups and downs followed before, in 1932, Cotton acquired an interest in a company that had discovered a comparatively simple method of producing colour transparencies. He realised that there would be a wide market for such a film, particularly in the rapidly expanding cinematograph industry, providing that the basic film stock could be developed to give improved definition. With characteristic drive, Cotton set about the task. How he achieved success, and the story of the rise and fall of the Dufaycolor Company, has no place here.

It was, however, because of his international travels for the Dufaycolor Company that, at about the time of the Munich crisis, Sidney Cotton received an approach from French intelligence sources. Would he, they asked, be prepared to take part in clandestine photographic reconnaissance operations for the Allied cause?

That such information was needed in time of peace may seem strange. In fact, as the year 1938 neared its end, detailed information of military dispositions and installations in Europe had become a matter of supreme importance.

In March of that year, Adolf Hitler had used propaganda and threats to seize Austria for the German nation. With the coming of Autumn—under the pretext of protecting German-speaking inhabitants of the Sudeten area of Czechoslovakia—he sought to achieve a further expansion of the Third Reich. In an attempt to cool-down this explosive situation, Britain, France and Italy—without consulting the Czechoslovak government—ceded to Germany the predominantly German-speaking areas of Bohemia and Moravia.

The statesmen of Britain and France, who still believed that international problems could and should be settled by diplomatic means, were no match for Germany's Nazi leader. By the Spring of 1939 he had seized the remainder of Czechoslovakia and, despite his assurance of no more territorial claims in Europe, it was clear that no reliance could be attached to his words.

War in Europe, however dire the consequences, seemed almost inevitable, and intelligence reports intimated that there was little time left for preparations. Britain and France needed urgently first-class reconnaissance photographs of military installations in Germany, Italy and the Middle East. The requirement was easy to see: its fulfilment was an entirely different matter.

In the 1930s—and disregarding the activities of Adolf Hitler—international boundaries still had a real meaning. They were not treated with the scant respect that is more usual to-day. Furthermore, the state-of-the-art at that period could not provide aircraft capable of overflying a potential enemy's territory at such height and speed that their interception was virtually impossible. Intrusion into an enemy's airspace could only add fuel to an already-smouldering international situation. How, then, to gain the all-essential photographic coverage?

The only feasible solution was to utilise the services of a civilian owner/pilot, well-known in European circles who, under the cover of legitimate business flights could—by considerable risk and subterfuge—obtain the necessary photographs during his trips to and from the continent of Europe.

These were the circumstances in which Sidney Cotton was approached. Since the project appealed to his aviation, photographic and adventurous interests, he accepted without hesitation.

How to set about it?

The greatest problem of all had been resolved automatically when Cotton was chosen for the job, for he had a legitimate and near-perfect cover. The development of new market outlets for Dufaycolor provided sufficient reason for business trips in and around Europe and the Middle East.

Another important requirement was a suitable aircraft that must be used so frequently on bona fide flights that its passage to and from a variety of international airports would exercise no comment.

What was a suitable aircraft? This was a matter that required careful consideration. Range, payload and reliability were all-important. True, the French had already used civil light aircraft to make short-range penetrations of German airspace: with these they had gained some useful photographic coverage of Rhineland areas. What was needed now was a longer-range type, commensurate with Cotton's executive status. His choice was a Lockheed Model 12A Electra, a low-wing monoplane powered by two reliable air-cooled radial engines. Having made a decision he lost little time in obtaining one from America.

One other important requirement was a co-pilot upon whom he could rely implicitly; not only in respect of his ability as a pilot, but in the far more devious matters in which they would soon be engaged. Cotton's contact in British intelligence suggested a Canadian, named Bob Niven, who was nearing the end of a short-service commission in the RAF.

Niven proved to be a good choice; keen, adventurous and a capable pilot. Many flights were made with him in the co-pilot's seat as they set out to establish a pattern of frequent Continental transits. By the time that their arrivals and departures had become commonplace, Cotton had discovered that they worked well as a team and was satisfied that Niven was the man for the job. It remained only to discover whether he would be prepared to play a part in the dangerous game of aerial espionage. To Cotton's considerable relief, Bob Niven gave the simple and direct answer—yes.

It was then February 1939, and the moment had arrived to prove whether or not all the preparatory work had been worthwhile. Unfortunately, the initial attempts were more musical comedy than cloak and dagger.

Since the impending operations had been financed by the French intelligence service, the initial sorties were to be flown from Toussous-le-Noble. The plan was to photograph Mannheim and its surrounding areas. A big task needed a big camera, reasoned the French, and the first operation bordered on the ridiculous as attempts were made to load the camera at Toussous. By the time it was on board, Cotton was convinced that the object of their flight would be apparent to the dimmest spectator; but, concealing his thoughts, he soon had the Lockheed airborne.

Apart from a few moments of panic when, well into German territory, it appeared that a fighter aircraft was climbing to intercept them, the flight passed without incident, and it was assumed that useful coverage of Mannheim and parts of the Siegfried Line would have resulted.

Several more flights were made during the ensuing days, but Cotton was far from happy with the progress being made, especially when—under the fatuous plea of security—the French refused to allow him to see the resulting photographs. This was completely useless: how could he possibly judge the effectiveness of the flights? When, after several angry demands, he finally gained reluctant permission to see the results, he was disappointed to find that there were wide gaps in the coverage.

Suggestions of how to improve matters fell on deaf ears. They—the French—knew all there was to know about photo-reconnaissance: he—Cotton—was the amateur, whom they had chosen because of his cover and ability to fly an aircraft. Cotton's reaction was predictable. Contacting British intelligence, he refused to have anything more to do with the French. After one more flight, the Lockheed was left in France and he and Niven returned to London.

He then proposed the acquisition of a new Lockheed, to be operated with and for British intelligence sources. Receiving agreement, he lost no time in obtaining the machine and, when this arrived in England, he arranged for a number of modifications to enable the aircraft to fulfil its clandestine role more effectively. They involved the installation of additional petrol tanks to increase range, fitment of a self-designed pear-drop blister window on the port side of the cabin—enabling the pilot to have a sight of the ground beneath the aircraft—and the provision of an overall paint scheme of duck-egg blue that would make the aircraft difficult to see from below.

In this form the Lockheed was still a perfectly respectable civil aircraft: to carry out the operations for which it was intended it needed suitable cameras. Cotton devised an arrangement of three RAF F24 cameras, so aligned that when flying at 20,000ft (6,100m) it would be possible to photograph a strip some ten miles (16km) wide below the aircraft's track. Operated by remote control from the pilot's cockpit, they were mounted in the cabin floor and concealed by almost undetectable sliding panels in the under-fuselage. In addition, a specially-modified Leica camera was mounted in each wing: a remote control concealed beneath the pilot's seat enabled under-wing panels to slide aside and the cameras to blink their eyes at the scene unfolding below.

To complete the preparations, some battered and weary-looking pieces of baggage were acquired. Liberally bespattered with the labels of international travel, they seemed a conspicuous and unlikely hiding place for anything so damning as reconnaissance cameras, their accessories and spares.

By June 1939 the Lockheed had been flight tested in its new form. Once again, Cotton and Niven were ready to start their adventures.

First task was a series of flights to and around the Middle East, and on June 14th 1939 the Lockheed was *en-route* to Malta. The initial job was coverage of Sicily, and the excellent photographs obtained satisfied Cotton that all was well with the photographic arrangements. Next leg of the flight was to Cairo; and defences, gun emplacements and new military installations at Leros gave up their secrets to the Lockheed's hidden eyes. Rhodes, too, could not conceal a concentration of naval craft and a new airfield under construction.

The entire flight, covering later the borders of the Red Sea, was almost without event. Almost! Labourers were refuelling the Lockheed at Atbara from four-gallon cans when a sandstorm blew up. Horrified at the possibility of sand infiltration into the aircraft's tanks, despite use of a filter funnel, and worried also by the fact that it was taking so long to refuel that he might not gain Cairo before dark, Cotton calculated a minimum fuel load. He decided that an imprudent 25 per cent margin for the flight to Cairo would suffice and called a halt at that point.

Soon after take-off the Lockheed was bucking into a headwind, and it rapidly became apparent that a forced-landing in the desert was a distinct possibility. With engines throttled back to the limit, the aircraft clawed its way through the air while Cotton tried every permutation of fuel management to eke out the diminishing supply. By the time that Almaza became discernible in the fading light, fuel gauges were reading empty. With sighs of relief from both pilots, the Lockheed's wheels rumbled a soothing sound of safety. Checks showed that the fuel tanks were almost bone dry: it had been a close call.

Now they were ready for the main task—photographic reconnaissance of German military installations.

The most difficult problem was to make a perfectly normal business contact in Germany, so that flights could be made to and from that country without arousing any suspicions. In this matter luck played a leading role.

Back in England after the Middle East trip, Cotton received a telephone call from a business associate telling him that Herr Schoene—a German—was interested in acquiring sales rights for Dufaycolor. This was exactly the lead he needed and, with the approach coming from the other side of the Channel, no suspicion of his actions would arise. He could not, of course, dismiss from his mind the possibility that details of his plans might have leaked out.

This latter factor, more than anything else, dictated a cautious approach that was really out of character. He decided that the first move was to invite Schoene to London to discuss his proposals and the potential markets for Dufaycolor.

The German, when he arrived in England some days later, was found to have much in common with Cotton, and this helped to encourage a mutual feeling of confidence. It appeared that he, too, had been a pilot: in fact, he had been a member of the famous Richthofen squadron in World War I, during which time he had become friendly with the man who was now Reichsmarschall Hermann Goering, the German Air Minister. Despite this friendship, Schoene professed to be an anti-Nazi, and Cotton was soon convinced that this was a most suitable contact for his purposes. Appointing him as the company's German agent, he proceeded to play the fish very carefully.

It was not until late in July that he received, and accepted, an invitation to visit Berlin. This initial visit was to be made as a perfectly legitimate business trip, without any attempt to secure reconnaissance photographs,

The Russian MiG–23 reconnaissance aircraft; so fast that no other combat aeroplane can catch it.

(Overleaf) French observation balloon at the Battle of Fleurus, on June 26th 1794. The pilot and observer were equipped with a spy-glass and signal flag. /*Royal Aeronautical Society.*

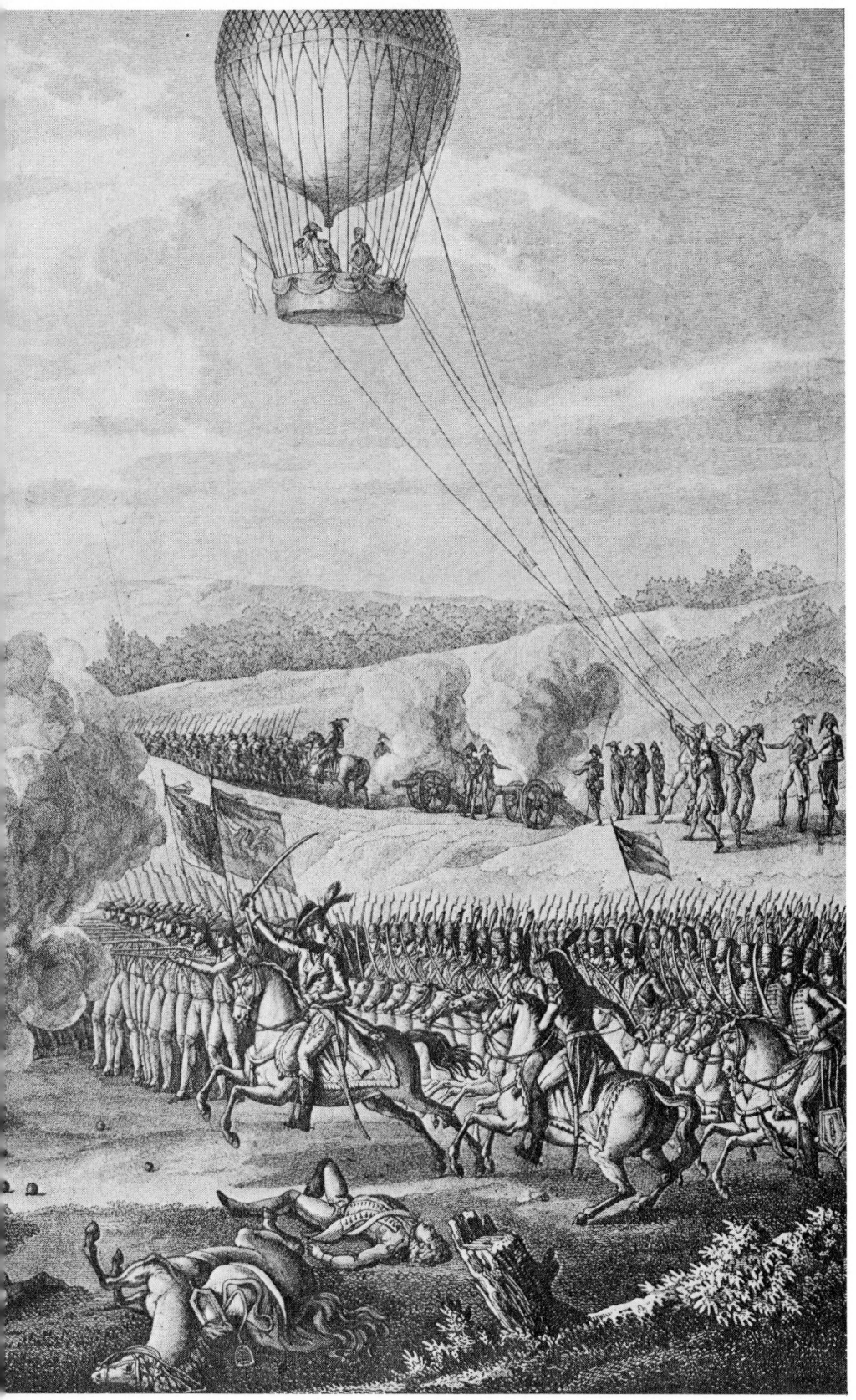

Inflation of the balloon *Intrepid* during the American Civil War battle of Fair Oaks, May 31st–June 1st 1862. /USAF

A balloon being packed by the Balloon Section of the Royal Engineers on Laffan's Plain, Farnborough, about 1894. /IWM

(Above) RNAS Coastal type non-rigid airship over a first World War convoy. Airships of this type were used for patrols off Lands End, the mouths of the Humber and the Forth, north of Aberdeen and off the Norfolk coast. /IWM

(Left) A typical Drachen kite-balloon of the RNAS. Those used over the Western Front in France were equipped with telephone, map-rest and static-line parachutes.

(Below) SS (Sea Scout) airship, with a car similar to the fuselage of a Maurice Farman aeroplane. Such craft were used to search for enemy submarines and surface ships in the narrow seas.

Twenty-seven C (Coastal) non-rigid airships entered service, from 1915. Endurance was eleven hours at 45mph. This one is refuelling experimentally from a cruiser.

A crew of three was carried in the B.E.2b aircraft-type car of the SS 14 airship.

German Zeppelin rigid airships were the ultimate in lighter-than-air military aircraft. Each was reckoned to be worth five or six naval cruisers in keeping track of Allied shipping movements. /P. J. R. Moyes

The RFC's first reconnaissance flight, by Capt Joubert de la Ferté, flying a Blériot XI*bis* monoplane, and Lt G. W. Mapplebeck in a B.E.2b, August 19th 1914. /*from painting by Kenneth McDonough*

(Left) Early power-driven camera used by the RFC, showing airscrew-powered flexible drive-shaft.

(Right) Reconnaissance camera mounted on side of observer's cockpit of an RFC F.E.2d aircraft.

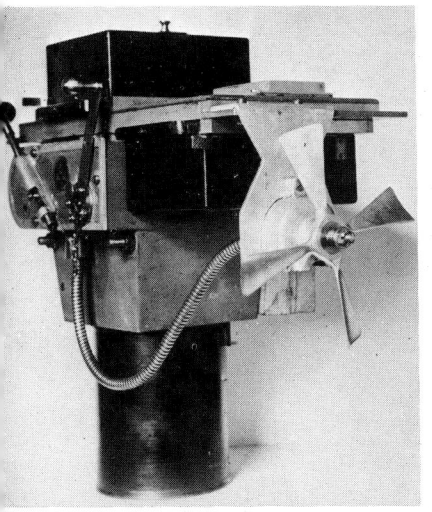
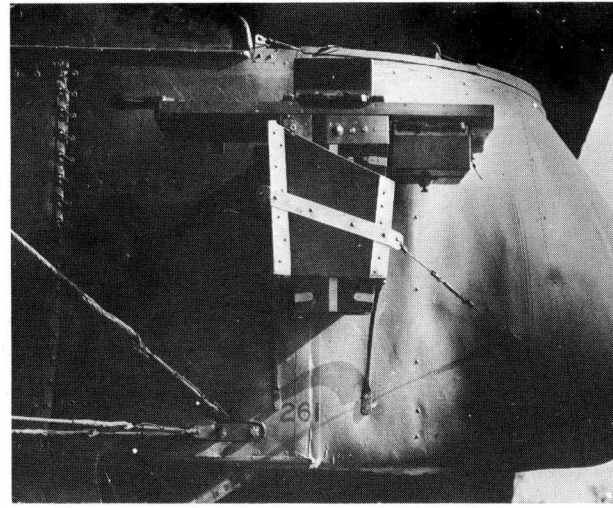

More than twenty years' progress in reconnaissance aircraft is reflected in the photographs on this page. Below are two of the R.E.8s which circled endlessly over the trenches in France, observing and correcting the fire of Allied artillery. The crew of the Lysander aircraft of World War II (right) had a far more modern camera, here being installed, and a more comfortable enclosed cockpit.

but it was still fraught with danger. As the Lockheed banked into the approach to Tempelhof Airport, both Cotton and Niven realised that their pulses were racing.

Cotton levelled the Lockheed off, throttled back the engines and, too soon for peace of mind, the wheels touched the airport's surface. As they taxied in they realised, with horror, that a squad of Nazi storm troopers was doubling towards them. Was it all over before it had begun? Had they been the poor fish to swallow a cunningly-devised Nazi bait? There was nothing to do but face it out.

When the storm troopers formed a guard of honour, both Cotton and Niven felt that the sudden relief from their guilt complex must be apparent to all. But no. A smiling Herr Schoene was there to greet them, and before long they had been swept away in ostentatious saloon cars.

The Lockheed had, meanwhile, been placed in a special hangar, and it did little for Cotton's peace of mind that night to discover that it came under the jurisdiction of the Gestapo. He felt certain that the aircraft would be gone over with a fine tooth-comb. Would they find the secret camera panels? Would any other tell-tale evidence alert them to the aircraft's true role? These, and countless other questions tortured his mind as he endeavoured to maintain the front of a suave and unruffled business executive.

The following morning test shots were made with film samples that Cotton had brought to Berlin and, that afternoon, he and Niven took off again for London, promising to return to Frankfurt on the following day, after the negative film had been developed and processed.

The moment of truth had arrived.

Despite the distinct possibility that they were putting their heads into a trap, it was decided to install the two Leica cameras in the wing mountings before setting out for Frankfurt. If, during the Lockheed's overnight stay in Berlin, the concealing panels had been discovered, it was almost certain that a further examination would be made at Frankfurt and the damning evidence revealed.

It was a calculated risk that had to be taken if they were to achieve the results for which so many preparations had been made.

Accordingly, at about noon on July 28th, the Lockheed was taxied out from Heston for take-off. Soon they were in the air, heading for Frankfurt via Brussels, where Cotton had arranged to pick up an Australian who wanted to visit an international air meet that was taking place at Frankfurt.

Cotton had hoped that the stop at Brussels might enable him to divert a little from his direct flight path to Frankfurt, so providing an opportunity for some photographic coverage of the Siegfried Line *en-route*. Brussels, however, caused his mind to be fogged with question marks, for he was given strict instructions to follow a route to Frankfurt that would keep him well clear of the Siegfried Line. What had been discovered? How much did they know? What would be the reception at Frankfurt?

Might as well be hung for sheep as lambs, they decided, and allowed the Lockheed to stray as far as might seem accidentally possible from the authorised route, thus gaining some photographs. They resolved to fill in the gaps on the return trip—if there was a return trip!

When they taxied in at Frankfurt, Schoene was there to welcome Cotton, and it was apparent from his manner that, so far at any rate, the clandestine purposes of the Lockheed had not been discovered.

The air meet at Frankfurt was primarily for light aircraft. By contrast, the Lockheed 12A towered above them, and was a subject of general interest, to the extent that the Commandant of Tempelhof, a visitor to the air meet, asked Cotton if he might have a flight in the American aircraft.

This, decided Cotton, was too good an opportunity to miss. He agreed immediately, and countered with the suggestion that, if permitted, he would welcome an opportunity to overfly the Mannheim area. This, he explained, was because he had never yet had an opportunity to see from the air the beautiful views of the Rhine of which he had heard so much.

Almost to his surprise permission was granted and, on the following day, one of the most fantastic reconnaissance sorties ever recorded entered the annals of aviation history. With the Commandant of Tempelhof sitting beside him in the co-pilot's seat, Cotton activated the Leica cameras and captured for British intelligence superb views of many new airfields and military installations that dotted the countryside some 2,000ft (610m) below the all-seeing eyes of his—ironically German-made—Leica cameras.

The event passed without incident and, when the air meet ended, he and Niven took off from Frankfurt *en-route* for London. Despite detailed instructions of the course to follow, they decided that areas of cloud on the prescribed route would provide sufficient excuse for 'losing their way'. Thus, they were able to take a first-class series of photographs of the Siegfried Line before breaking off into Belgium.

It was not until mid-August that an opportunity arose to make photographic coverage of airfields adjacent to Berlin. When Cotton taxied in at Tempelhof afterwards, Schoene's expression told him immediately that his circuitous route was suspect. It was fortunate that Schoene had some influence for, seizing upon an excuse proffered by Cotton, he was able to divert the authorities from making further enquiries.

It was at about this time, when it became clear that the issue of war or peace in Europe hinged upon whether or not Hitler launched his armed might against Poland, that Cotton had one of his 'ideas'.

He came to the conclusion that war might be averted if the Nazi leaders were convinced that Britain would take up arms in support of Poland. If, he conjectured, Goering could be induced to visit England as his guest, it might be possible to convince him of Britain's determination. Then he, in turn, might dissuade Hitler from signalling the start of what must inevitably become the second World War.

The invitation, tendered through Schoene, was accepted and Cotton learned that Goering had set the date for his visit—August 24th.

With this information, Cotton lost no time in returning to London, and immediately advised British intelligence of what he had done. Rather to his surprise the idea was welcomed, and arrangements were made for informal talks between Goering and certain ministers.

On August 22nd Cotton and Niven took the Lockheed back to Berlin, prepared to pick up their guest on August 24th. By this time, however, tension was beginning to mount in Berlin, and there was little doubt that the situation between Germany and Poland was nearing a climax. On the following day Cotton was told that Goering's visit to London was cancelled, and he decided that it was desirable to return home as quickly as possible if he and Niven were to escape internment.

Next morning they arrived early at Tempelhof, only to discover that they could not get authorisation to take off. Anxious and frustrated, they climbed into the Lockheed and taxied to a take-off position; but a succession of signals from the control tower left little doubt that any attempt to take-off without permission would almost certainly result in disaster.

They stopped the engines and sat waiting. Minutes ticked off slowly and painfully as they chewed their fingers and kept looking at apparently unmoving wrist-watches. Almost an hour had passed when a car came speeding towards them across the airfield. One of its occupants was Schoene, who assured Cotton that every effort was being made to get permission for them to leave.

The car hurried away. Another interminable period of waiting followed: by the time half-an-hour had passed, Cotton was almost at the point of attempting to take off, and to hell with the consequences.

Suddenly, they could see the car returning. This time it brought the necessary permission. A detailed route was handed to Cotton and, on this occasion, he considered it prudent to obey. Within minutes the Lockheed's wheels trundled over Tempelhof's surface for the last time. They had escaped.

Characteristically, it took little time for both Cotton and Niven to regain their reconnaissance professionalism. The panels covering the Leicas were soon withdrawn and, although maintaining the prescribed course, both pilots were alert for any useful detail that might be recorded.

The Lockheed, in its clandestine operations, had enabled British intelligence to acquire hundreds of valuable reconnaissance photographs. This late homecoming flight from Germany was no exception, for anchored in the Schillig Roads, near Wilhelmshaven, major units of the German Fleet were recorded by the little Leica cameras.

The prints, when presented to the Admiralty, caused some excitement. There was an immediate request for photographic coverage of other important targets and, considering the risk of interception to be only marginal, Cotton agreed to see what he could do.

This time there was no need for the subterfuge that had been necessary on the trips to Berlin, and the Lockheed fairly bristled with cameras. The only snag was that there were more than Cotton and Niven could operate, if the aircraft was to be kept in the air. So, for the first time since their early flight for French intelligence, they carried a volunteer camera operator.

When they took off on August 27th, the flight plan called for coverage of Borkum, Nordeney, Heligoland and Sylt. Things were going along quite smoothly until, as they were approaching Nordeney, a German fighter came hurtling towards them in what appeared to be a head-on attack. Cotton and Niven exchanged glances: was the partnership to be dissolved now? The German machine swept past, without firing its guns. Anti-climax. He had either ignored them or failed to see them.

Wilhelmshaven was the first photographic target offered to Cotton after Germany invaded Poland on September 1st, and this time Niven made a solo sortie in a four-seat light aircraft that Cotton had owned for some time. This, too, was highly successful, and when presented with the photographic evidence the First Sea Lord was rather staggered to learn that this vital material had been supplied by a civilian pilot flying an unarmed civil aircraft.

Naval Intelligence was the next customer, anxious to discover whether refuelling facilities for enemy U-boats were in existence along the neutral shores of Southern Ireland. This was a job for the Lockheed, and Cotton and Niven made a series of sorties, providing photographic evidence that no such facilities existed.

It was not long before news of Cotton's reconnaissance successes came to the ears of the Air Ministry, and he was requested to pay a visit to Air Vice-Marshal Peck. Coming to the interview with some trepidation, and searching his mind for some clue as to what terrible crime he had committed against the Royal Air Force, he was relieved to find that it was his advice that was being sought.

At a time when the RAF was having extreme difficulty in obtaining worthwhile reconnaissance photographs, despite use of the most modern equipment available, it was not only something of a mystery, but also rather galling, that a civilian should be stealing its thunder.

What, the officers wanted to know, was the secret of his success? What new and revolutionary equipment was producing the results that had, so far, eluded their well-trained crews? It came as something of a shock to learn that his equipment was similar to that used by the RAF.

Suggestions that he might give the Air Force the benefit of his experience did not fall on deaf ears; but Cotton was convinced that it would be better for him to have service backing to develop the facilities already in existence at Heston, rather than join the RAF and, in his view, start from scratch.

Other meetings followed, but it was soon apparent that this Admiralty-sponsored civilian had little appeal to the RAF. The age-old inter-service conflict was beginning to rear its ugly head again. There was approval when he agreed to assist in obtaining reconnaissance photographs of German naval movements off the Dutch coast; but the mood changed rapidly to consternation when he requested the use of a service aircraft in which to make his own reconnaissance sortie.

A further meeting was planned for the following day, but Cotton had already decided that shock tactics were necessary if any progress was to be made. Locating Bob Niven without delay, he arranged for the Lockheed to be got ready. Before long they were in the air and, using clearance techniques learned during the earlier reconnaissance sorties for the Admiralty, the Lockheed was soon heading out over the Kent coast. The flight was made without incident and, on return, a late-night session ensured that the films were developed and enlargements made ready for the next day.

When Cotton reported to the Air Ministry on the following morning he had a bulging briefcase. The meeting followed a similar indeterminate course to those which had preceded it. When Cotton considered that discussion had droned on for long enough, he presented his collection of prints to A. V-M. Peck.

There was no doubt that Peck was impressed. The clarity and detail of the enlargements was exactly what the RAF had sought to achieve. He intimated as much, adding that it was impossible, of course, to draw a fair comparison between reconnaissance photographs taken under the ideal and leisurely conditions of peacetime and the hasty, sly peeps that were imposed by war. Purely as a matter of academic interest, he enquired when they had been taken.

Cotton's reply, to the effect that they had been secured on the previous afternoon, brought an immediate, stunned silence. It lasted for only an instant of time: then came an uproar from the entire assembly, shocked at the outrageous behaviour of this dreadful man. It seemed to Cotton that he was in danger of imminent arrest, so he took advantage of the chaos to disappear quietly from the scene.

Despite the injury to pride and sensibilities, the RAF was astute enough to appreciate that Cotton had succeeded where its own methods had failed. It needed, however, the calm approach of the Chief of Air Staff to convince Cotton of the RAF's need to avail itself of his know-how.

From this strange beginning came a new approach to photo-reconnaissance. It was to become a vital component of the junior service: one that was to have far-reaching consequences in the war years that lay ahead.

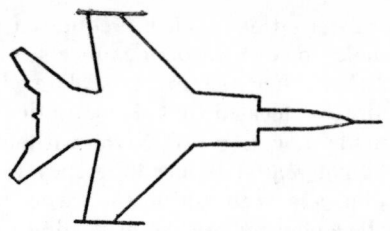

# 4 How to Win the War

Sidney Cotton was not the only person who realised the vital importance of photo-reconnaissance. In Germany, Colonel-General Baron von Fritsch predicted, just before it started, that: "The next war will be won by the military organisation with the most efficient photographic reconnaissance". Although he spoke with authority, as a former commander-in-chief of the German army, it is often suggested that his opposite numbers of the *Luftwaffe*, far from sharing his extreme view, regarded air photography as little more than an incidental adjunct to the role of army co-operation squadrons.

This may be true in terms of tactical reconnaissance; strategically, the *Luftwaffe* seems to have been more enlightened. Captured vertical photographs and charts, dated October 2nd 1939, show that by then the German bomber crews were being assisted by up-to-the-minute information on most of their potential targets in the UK. Docks, bridges, fuel storage tanks and anti-aircraft gun positions are all carefully annotated. Most interesting of all are photographs of places like St Abbs Head, which show Britain's radar stations clearly marked as worthwhile targets.

Fortunately, the Germans underestimated the decisive part that radar would play in conserving the strength and directing the aim of RAF Fighter Command in the Battle of Britain. As their air offensive gathered momentum, on August 12th 1940, they concentrated on weakening the defences. Five of the precious radar stations were hit so hard that the *Luftwaffe* felt confident that they would play no further part in the battle. In fact, only the Isle of Wight installation had been destroyed; the others were all operational on the following day.

Reichsmarschall Hermann Goering, supreme commander of the *Luftwaffe*, was irritated but not greatly perturbed. If the radars were more difficult to knock out than had been anticipated, there was little point in wasting effort in repeated attacks on them. With Fighter Command well on the way to being eliminated, the radars would have no value in any case.

Efficient reconnaissance over RAF airfields might have prevented General Stapf from reporting on August 13th that eight British air bases had been destroyed and that the RAF was losing three aircraft for every *Luftwaffe* machine shot down, the ratio for fighter losses being five to one.

Such miscalculations helped to decide the outcome of the Battle of Britain.

The RAF was making equally poor use of air photography. Despite the lessons of World War I, it had simply packed vertical or oblique cameras into aircraft of various types, from Lysanders to Blenheims, in the late 'thirties, without any real concept of how the equipment should best be used. A few briefless and bewildered photo interpreters found their way to the Continent with RAF squadrons in 1940; but there is nothing to suggest that air intelligence had any impact on the campaign that ended with the enemy installed down the full length of the Channel coast.

Safe behind its own still-secret Chain Home line of radar stations, Britain felt smug at having a defensive system without any counterpart on the other side of the Channel. Her leaders ought to have known better after the events of December 14th 1939.

On that day, twelve Wellingtons of No 99 Squadron set out in daylight to attack German naval targets near Wilhelmshaven and Heligoland. They came under heavy attack from enemy fighters and anti-aircraft guns over the Schillig Roads, and lost half their number. Four days later, a force of 22 Wellingtons from Nos 9, 37 and 149 Squadrons found Bf 109 and Me 110 fighters waiting for them in great strength in the same area. No bombs could be dropped, as all enemy ships sighted were in harbour and there was a strict embargo on attacks which might cause civilian casualties. In contrast, ten Wellingtons were shot down, two more had to ditch in the sea, and three others were destroyed in forced-landings.

Even after this, it was not appreciated that the enemy fighters were in the right place because they were being directed by radar, which located and tracked the incoming bombers.

It was nearly one year later that a sharp-eyed photo interpreter spotted two tiny circular objects in the corner of a French field, on a photograph brought back by a camera-carrying Spitfire. Three months later, on February 22nd 1941, a daring low-level flight over the same spot produced the first close-up pictures of German *Freya* radars, corresponding to the long-range British Chain Home stations.

The shocked surprise of such a discovery was made worse later in 1941. Intelligence reports suggested that the enemy had a counterpart to British Gun-laying and Ground Controlled Interception sets, and that this was being used to control his night fighter force. With RAF Bomber Command building up for a massive non-stop night offensive, it was essential to discover whether or not these so-called *Würzburg* sets really existed.

What had first looked like a speck of dust on a photograph of a *Freya* site at Bruneval, near Le Havre, suddenly took a more sinister significance. *Würzburg* was said to be located near existing long-range radars, and that 'speck' demanded closer inspection.

Before there was time to put a request through official channels, a PR pilot named Sqn Ldr Tony Hill heard about the suspicious dot on a photograph and decided, unofficially, to uncover the truth. Racing at treetop height over Bruneval, he saw what looked like a large electric bowl-fire.

His camera failed to work, but Hill's description seemed to confirm the worst fears of the radar experts.

Just to make sure, Hill decided to take a second look at the installation on the following day. Again it was an unofficial sortie, and as he prepared for take-off someone told him that three pilots from a rival squadron had been ordered to take photographs in the Bruneval area at the same time. Undeterred, he taxied his Spitfire over to where the others were waiting to go, and told the startled pilots that if he found any of them within 20 miles (32km) of 'his target' he would shoot them down.

The close-up photographs of *Würzburg* that he took soon afterwards— unmolested by other RAF pilots—convinced Britain's war leaders that they must learn the precise capabilities of this German apparatus. So, on the night of February 27/28th 1942, a company of paratroops was dropped over Bruneval by the Whitley bomber-transports of No 51 Squadron. With them went Flt Sgt C. W. H. Cox, an RAF radar mechanic, who calmly dismantled key parts of the *Würzburg* while the paratroops fought off enemy soldiers.

Their work finished, the British force blew up what was left of the apparatus and withdrew to the beach, where the Navy was waiting to pick them up.

In the first volume of the official history of the part played by the RAF in World War II,* Denis Richards commented: "At the small cost of fifteen casualties—and the Germans suffered many more—we were thus able to improve our acquaintance with a vital element in the German air defences. The result was that we could apply our counter-measures, such as jamming, or low flying, or 'saturation' by large numbers of aircraft, with all the greater effect. Another victory had been recorded in the 'radio war', that ceaseless battle of wits which was to determine the future of our bombing offensive, and with it the course of the whole titanic conflict."

By this time Britain had a powerful new ally fighting by her side. On December 7th 1941, the Japanese had struck a devastating blow against Pearl Harbor, and America was at war. In due course, this was to make possible a 'round-the-clock' bomber offensive in Europe, with the RAF attacking by night and the US Army Air Forces by day. The Allied propaganda machine predicted the rapid collapse of Nazi Germany under such a hammering. Only those with access to photographs of Bomber Command's targets, taken after its raids, felt nagging doubts.

What had begun in 1939 with the cloak-and-dagger exploits of Sidney Cotton was now a science of ever-increasing scope and importance. The first specialised RAF photo-reconnaissance unit had come into being at Heston aerodrome within three weeks of the start of the war. Its leader was Cotton, now a slightly reluctant Squadron Leader, and its equipment included two Spitfires, wheeled out of Fighter Command only by great perseverance.

* *Royal Air Force 1939–45* (HMSO; 1953).

Painted pale green and belonging officially to an organisation called the Special Survey Flight, to hide its true purpose, Spitfire N3071 had been based at Seclin, near Lille, in November 1939. Soon it was flying at a height of 33,000ft (10,000m) over enemy ports, manufacturing centres and Germany's Siegfried Line defences, bringing back photographs packed full of valuable information but so tiny in scale that nobody could interpret what they revealed. Nobody, that is, except Major 'Lemnos' Hemming, who put the photos in a huge Wild photogrammetric machine belonging to his civilian air survey company and proved that it would even be possible to count, measure and identify ships of the German fleet at their home bases by using such techniques.

Out of Cotton's small Photographic Development Unit grew the Photographic Reconnaissance Unit (PRU), as an integral part of RAF Coastal Command, in July 1940. With the enemy invasion fleet massing in the Channel ports, its pilots were kept extremely busy. Every new arrival, every smallest move, had to be observed and evaluated instantly. If the weather was too cloudy for high-altitude photography, the Spitfire pilots had to go in 'on the deck', at sea level, a type of flying that was referred to as 'dicing' after somebody had made a bad joke about 'dicing with death'.

Maryland bombers, fitted with cameras, handled PR work from Malta, providing the photographs on which the Fleet Air Arm planned its spectacular attack against the Italian fleet in harbour at Taranto, on November 11th 1940. Hurricanes and Beaufighters followed in the Middle East, and Mosquitoes in Britain.

Meanwhile, a unit known as No 3 PRU had come into being at RAF Oakington, near Cambridge, as part of Bomber Command. It soon abandoned its original task of using Spitfires to photograph targets that had been attacked by RAF bombers, in order to assess the degree of destruction that had been achieved. Instead, it concentrated on improving the technique of night reconnaissance by means of flash-bombs, and on the interpretation of photographs taken by the bombers themselves.

Since the beginning of the bomber offensive, crews had returned with stories of smashed and burning targets. Their claims were often confirmed by neutral persons who had travelled in Germany; but the photographs taken by cameras inside the bombers told a very different story.

In theory, these cameras were supposed to take their pictures at the precise moment when the flash-bombs exploded and the bombs were on their way to the target. In fact, when the PRU staff at Oakington studied 151 flashlight photographs taken in three months during the Winter of 1940–41, not more than 21 showed the target areas.

How should such disastrous facts be used? Intelligence officers in Nos 3 and 5 Groups, from whose aircraft the pictures were taken, were unable to prevent the news spreading. Some crews, confident of their navigation, refused to believe the evidence. Others, realising the truth, became depressed, feeling that all the effort and sacrifice of life was wasted. One natural reaction was that crews began to detest the equipment on board their aircraft that was supposed to help them but merely highlighted their apparent failure.

A further careful assessment was made later that year by a team of statisticians headed by Professor Lindemann (later Lord Cherwell), at the personal instigation of Prime Minister Winston Churchill. Based on photographs taken during June and July 1941, their conclusions were that only one aircraft in three had made its attack within five miles (8km) of its designated target. Over the heavily defended Ruhr, the average fell to one aircraft in ten.

In his history of *The Second World War*, Churchill wrote: "The air photographs showed how little damage was being done. It also appeared that the crews knew this, and were discouraged by the poor results of so much hazard. Unless we could improve on this there did not seem much use in continuing night bombing."

As on so many occasions when British air power has been threatened, industry and science came to the rescue. Less than a fortnight after the Bruneval raid, Bomber Command began using on a large scale a radio navigation aid known as 'Gee'. This enabled an aircrew to fix their position over the target within one mile (1.6km) by means of radio pulses transmitted from three widely-dispersed stations in England. It was followed by a second device, code-named 'Oboe', which was even more accurate but involved flying straight and level for a considerable time. This was not a healthy thing to do in a well-defended area; in addition, both 'Gee' and 'Oboe' were of limited range and could not be used to locate targets beyond the Ruhr valley.

$H_2S$ was different. Identified by a radar scanner spinning in a blister fairing under the belly of the bomber, it was self-contained. To-day, we take for granted radar that enables the navigator of an airliner to receive a constantly-changing TV-like 'map' of the terrain far beneath his aircraft, and that warns of high ground and even of stormy weather ahead. When $H_2S$ entered service in 1943, it was revolutionary. Requiring no ground signals, it could be used at any range from a bomber's base. Pathfinder squadrons of Bomber Command used it for precise location of targets, which were then marked with coloured flares at which the crews of the main force aimed their bombs. The results were truly devastating.

The combination of reconnaissance to select targets and the new radio and radar navigation aids to guide the attacking force gave Bomber Command the effectiveness it had lacked in 1939–41. No operation demonstrated this better than one which took place in the Summer of 1943.

For some time PR crews had been keeping special watch on mysterious activities at a place called Peenemünde on the western shores of the Baltic. Suspicions had first been aroused as early as May 15th 1942, when Flt Lt D. W. Steventon had made a routine sortie over the area, with Kiel and Swinemünde as his primary objectives. Like all good PR pilots, he was constantly on the look-out for anything new, and it seemed worthwhile to expose a little spare film as his Spitfire passed high over some strange-looking ring-shape constructions in woods near an airfield.

At RAF Medmenham in Buckinghamshire, home of the Photographic Interpretation Unit since early 1941, the photographs were studied briefly then put on one side. With so much of immediate importance to be done, by so few people, Peenemünde could wait.

So, in secret isolation, the German scientists and engineers led by Major-General Walter Dornberger and Dr Wernher von Braun were left to develop unhampered the *vergeltungswaffen* (reprisal weapons) on which Adolf Hitler relied to turn the tide of war in Europe.

With a roar like rolling thunder, a huge liquid-fuelled rocket weighing $13\frac{1}{2}$ tons lifted off the launch-pad inside one of those puzzling ring-structures at Peenemünde on October 3rd 1942. Accelerating to more than 3,000mph (4,800km/h) it became the first man-made object to travel into almost-airless space, before falling back to Earth 120 miles (195km) from its launch-point and only $2\frac{1}{2}$ miles (4km) from its theoretical target point. It hit the Earth with an impact energy which Dornberger described as being equivalent to that of fifty 100-ton railway locomotives all crashing into a wall simultaneously at 60mph (100km/h).

Operational use of the rocket, as the V2, was still nearly two years away. Meanwhile, other work progressed steadily. By December 1942, early versions of a small pilotless 'flying-bomb' missile were being air-launched from larger aircraft over Peenemünde. This was to be the V1, with a one-ton warhead contained in its pointed nose. And from the same airfield test pilot Heini Dittmar was flying prototypes of a tiny tailless rocket fighter known as the Me 163, which could far exceed all existing world speed records.

The story of how scraps of evidence about these fantastic weapons were gradually pieced together is one of the classics of wartime intelligence. Reports of the mysterious goings-on at Peenemünde reached England from agents and patriots among the conquered peoples of Europe. Polish freedom-fighters even managed to beat the enemy in recovering vital parts of a V2 rocket that went off course, fell into soft earth and was flown to Britain in one of the RAF Dakotas that took part in night operations in support of the 'underground' movement.

At Medmenham, every new photograph was examined minutely for details of the 'secret weapons' that were supposedly being perfected for use against England. When there was no longer any doubt of the key role that Peenemünde was playing in this work, Bomber Command was alerted for a single, massive strike. This took place on the night of August 17/18th 1943, when 597 aircraft dropped 1,937 tons of bombs over the relatively small experimental station. Led by Pathfinders, they achieved good results, but German fighters made full use of the bright moonlight that revealed the returning aircraft and forty bombers were shot down.

This was only the end of the first round of the battle of the V-weapons. Before long, Allied reconnaissance aircraft were bringing back photographs of an immense string of strangely-shaped installations which were code-named 'ski-sites'. It was soon realised that the ski-shaped buildings were intended for storage of V1 'flying-bomb' components. As the picture built up, it seemed likely that the enemy was planning to launch anything up to 2,000 of the robot weapons every 24 hours. Could even London withstand such an onslaught?

It never had to do so. With all the ski-sites identified and pin-pointed, they were subjected to devastating attacks by aircraft of the RAF and USAAF. By the beginning of 1944, all were flattened. Round three of the battle began when the actual launch-ramps began to be spotted, under construction all down the Pas de Calais and aimed at London. The new sites came under constant attack, but the V1 menace was not ended until Allied armies overran the launch area after D-Day.

Much more could be written about the part played by reconnaissance in World War II. The 'Dambusters' achieved their gallant, spectacular success because every detail of their difficult targets had been revealed by repeated PR sorties. The extent of their triumph was revealed by post-attack photographs in which even the least-skilled viewer could see the water pouring through an immense breach in the wall of the Moehne dam.

When the Allied armies went ashore on D-Day, the territory over which they fought their way inland was as familiar as their training grounds in Britain. Every inch had been photographed by PR aircraft, and the prints had been used as the basis for highly-accurate scale models of the beach-head areas. So that the points of attack would not be known to the enemy, equal attention had been paid to flying over and photographing other areas in which an invasion would have been practicable.

So, throughout the war, reconnaissance went on quietly, behind the scenes, improving steadily in capability and helping to make possible ultimate victory. Some of the final photographs were taken from B-29 bombers over Hiroshima and Nagasaki in Japan. The mushroom clouds that they recorded were from an entirely new and terrifying kind of weapon that left little in its shadow for anyone to photograph later.

As Colonel-General Baron von Fritsch had predicted, the side with the best photographic reconnaissance had won.

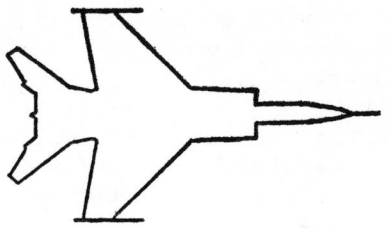

# 5 The Start of ECM

During the night of October 22nd/23rd 1943, the *Luftwaffe*'s night fighter pilots found another major problem added to the many with which they had to contend. Night after night the RAF was pounding the cities and war centres they were supposed to defend. To-night the target was Kassel.

In the three years since this accursed war had started—so successfully for Germany—their job had changed completely. With the *Freya* radars to guide them, it had been easy to find and pick off the fat-bellied, unescorted English Wellingtons that tried to bomb their navy in daylight, around Heligoland and Wilhelmshaven. Even when the RAF sought the cover of darkness for its attacks, interception had not been too difficult at first. Now it was different. Feint attacks often drew off the night fighters to entirely the wrong place. The bombers were armed with up to ten machine-guns in turrets which could provide a deadly deterrent to close-in attack; and sometimes the other aircraft proved to be a Mosquito intruder, with disastrous consequences for anyone who mistook it for a big, relatively slow and clumsy bomber.

Often it seemed that the only consolation was the friendly voice of the ground controller, whose job was to direct the night fighters towards the bomber force. Usually the voice was calm, as it could be when the speaker was seated in a warm and quiet room, in front of a radar screen on which the enemy was no more than a slowly moving 'blip' of light. Usually—but not to-night.

As the minutes ticked by, the messages over the fighter pilots' earphones became more and more excited and confused. Before long, they were chaotic. Clearly, there were now two precisely similar voices, one belonging to the real controller, the other to a 'ghost controller' whose sole aim was to mislead and confuse.

The furious German controller tried to warn the pilots under his command: "Don't be led astray by the enemy", and "In the name of General Schmid I order all aircraft to return to Kassel". As his patience wore thin, his outbursts grew in violence, and the 'ghost' remarked good-humouredly into his microphone: "The Englishman is now swearing". "Dammit", was the reply, "It's not the Englishman swearing, it's me!"

So began Operation Corona, under which a 'ghost controller' broadcast spoof messages to the German night fighter force over three of the GPO's high-power transmitters at Rugby. For the next six months, the lives of countless bomber crews were spared as the *Luftwaffe* was despatched to empty skies. For German fighter pilots, already having to contend with all the difficulties and hazards of night operations against a resolute enemy, it was demoralising. Worst of all was when the weather suddenly changed or the time came to return to base with barely adequate fuel. A message then might order diversion to another airfield, because the home station was under attack or closed in by cloud. Was it true? Might not the new destination be the one under attack or weather-bound? In any case, was there enough fuel left in the fighter's tanks to reach the alternate?

Morale suffered so much that a false order by the 'ghost controller' for all night fighters to land at the nearest airfield was often used as an excuse to avoid further troubles.

Operation Corona represented but one, brief episode in a 'radio war' that was waged throughout the 1939–45 conflict and has continued to the present day. This particular war relies on radio and radar as its primary weapons, with guns, rockets and bombs available only in a support role. It is closely allied to other forms of reconnaissance, because 'spy-planes' and satellites are often the best means of probing and identifying the techniques and equipment available to a real or potential enemy.

Until July 1940, Germany had envisaged no need for a specialised night-fighter force. In that month, Goering ordered General Kammhuber to take over two squadrons of Messerschmitt Me 110s, one squadron of Dornier Do 17s and a handful of the new Junkers Ju 88s and learn to operate them in conjunction with the *Freya* early-warning radars.

*Freya* had been used for observation of the airspace over Czechoslovakia since the pre-war occupation of that country. Other sets had gone into service in Germany, each working in the 125 megacycles band and with a range of about 100 miles (160km). The tactics worked out by Kammhuber's small force entailed taking off as soon as the *Freyas* or *Flugwachen* acoustic listening posts located an incoming raid, and then orbiting radio beacons until individual bombers could be illuminated by searchlights. The system was known as *Helle Nachtjagd* (illuminated night fighting).

We know now that *Freya* began to be supplemented by *Würzburg* as early as October 1940. Although limited to a range of only 15 miles (24km) the new radar, working in the 570 megacycles band, had the advantage of giving the height of the target. It soon became the heart of the German defence system, used for GCI (ground controlled interception) guidance of night fighters, as a radar range-finder for anti-aircraft guns and as a director for searchlights.

The success of the new tactics is indicated by the fact that a fighter force which never exceeded 120 aircraft had accounted for 42 of the 72 RAF night bombers shot down by the end of 1940. The main weakness of the operations was their reliance on searchlights, which were ineffective during cloudy conditions. To offset this shortcoming, *Himmelbett* (four-poster bed) was conceived. This involved dividing the area to be defended into 'boxes' 50 miles wide and 10 miles deep (80 × 16km). Each box was then sub-divided into three sub-boxes, each containing a pair of *Würzburgs*. When a bomber entered any sub-box it was tracked by one of the radars; the other *Würzburg* tracked a convenient night fighter, and a ground controller then guided the interceptor towards its target by bringing together the two 'blips' on the radar screen until the fighter pilot was near enough to see his prey.

Losses among the bombers increased markedly after this, and Bomber Command had to find a way of hampering the enemy radars. Not until December 1942 were two jamming devices ready to be tested in action. One of them was Mandrel, which blotted out all 'blips' on *Freya's* viewing screen except those from targets less than 20 miles (32km) from the radar. The other was Tinsel, which made use of the fact that the FuG 10 HF communications radio used in German night fighters operated on the same frequency as the T1154/R1155 set carried by RAF bombers. All that the radio operator on the bomber had to do was sweep through his band of frequencies until he picked up the German fighter controller, and then back-tune his transmitter so that it broadcast the roar of one of the bomber's engines by means of a microphone inside the engine cowling.

Mandrel was fitted to 144 of the bombers which attacked Mannheim on December 6th 1942. It rendered the enemy early-warning radars totally ineffective and no *Luftwaffe* fighter found a target until 21 minutes after the French coast had been crossed. A fortnight later, German interceptors failed to make contact with a force attacking Duisburg until three minutes before the bombs began to fall. By then, part of the credit went to Tinsel, which played havoc with the attempts by German controllers to guide the fighters to their targets. Within a month, Bomber Command losses fell by more than a third.

Each move by the enemy to reduce the effects of the jamming was met by improvements to Mandrel; but the *Luftwaffe* had another interception aid of which little was known.

Back in July 1942, a British radio monitoring station had first picked up messages suggesting that *Luftwaffe* night fighters were using an airborne device known as Emil Emil. Signals were detected subsequently by a station in East Anglia, but the only way of confirming suspicions was by sending out 'ferret' aircraft. This was a dangerous task, as the 'ferret' had to act as bait, allowing itself to be located and attacked by the enemy interceptor, so that it could radio back to its base data on any signals picked up from the equipment carried by its attacker. With luck, it might then carry out evasive action and escape home.

The 'ferrets' belonged to No 1474 (Wireless Investigation) Flight. Seventeen times they ventured out over the Netherlands, trying to lure *Luftwaffe* fighters on to their scent, without success. On the eighteenth occasion, on December 3rd 1942, the 'ferret' Wellington was so badly shot up by an enemy night fighter that it crashed into the Channel. Before it did so, its crew told listeners at their base the details of the German equipment that they so badly needed to know.

Emil Emil was confirmed as an airborne radar. Its correct name was, in fact, FuG 202 *Lichtenstein BC*, built by Telefunken. It worked in the 490 megacycles band and had range limits of 200 yards to 2 miles (180m to 3.2km). The pilots of the Me 110s and Ju 88Cs to which it was first fitted disliked it intensely, because it required a massive aerial array on the aircraft's nose, reducing speed by about 25mph (40km/h). But their enthusiasm grew in pace with the successes they achieved.

Britain's Telecommunications Research Establishment lost no time in countering *Lichtenstein* once it had been identified. From April 26th 1943, a jammer code-named Ground Grocer went into action from a station near Lowestoft, the farthest-east place on the English coastline. It worked best when the enemy fighter equipped with *Lichtenstein* was flying towards it, and produced so much 'clutter' on the pilot's radar screen that effective interception range was reduced to 500 yards (450m) when the aircraft was 140 miles (225km) distant.

Ground Grocer was clearly of most value in protecting a returning bomber force, because of its directional limitations. Serrate, also developed by TRE and first deployed on the Beaufighters of No 141 Squadron in June 1943, was a very different proposition, because it picked up radar signals transmitted from *Lichtenstein* and enabled the fighters to home on the source.

Within three months the crews of No 141 shot down 23 enemy night fighters. Their effect on the night battles was out of all proportion to their score, as morale in the *Luftwaffe* squadrons took a severe jolt. It had been a dangerous-enough sport to stalk huge bombers which could hit back with concentrated fire from the Browning guns in their power-operated turrets. Now, sometimes, the stalker became the stalked, the would-be killer the victim. As the bomber's 'blip' came nearer on the *Lichtenstein* display, the comparative silence of the night sky was suddenly rent by a shattering burst from the four cannon and six machine-guns of a Beaufighter that had crept up unobserved from behind.

On other occasions the crew of a Beaufighter played a kind of 'ferret' role, allowing a German night fighter to detect and close on them, in the belief that their aircraft was an unsuspecting bomber. The nearness of the interceptor could be gauged to a nicety by means of the backward cover of the Beau's AI (airborne interception) radar. Just before it came within firing or visual range, the RAF pilot whipped round in a fast, tight turn, on to the tail of the German before the enemy pilot had time to realise his mistake.

The only immediate answer for the *Luftwaffe* was to use its *Lichtenstein* more sparingly. It still had the *Würzburg* ground radars to guide it—until July 24th 1943.

On that night, Bomber Command's primary target was Hamburg. It was

This photograph of a German *Wurzburg* radar, taken by a Spitfire pilot, triggered off the daring Brunewald raid by British parachutists.

Another result of Spitfire reconnaissance, this low-level photograph gave first proof that the German air defence forces were using radar, known as *Freya*.

One of Britain's Chain Home radar stations. Failure to destroy them cost the *Luftwaffe* dearly in the Battle of Britain. /IWM

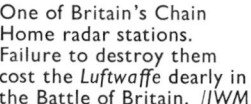

From the start of World War II *Luftwaffe* bomber crews had at their disposal superb target maps of most worthwhile objectives in the United Kingdom. The three documents reproduced on this page and opposite are typical. Above is a vertical aerial photograph of the RAF station at Scampton in Lincolnshire, dated October 1940. Opposite (top) is an annotated map of the same area, with hangars, bomb dumps and fuel tanks all clearly marked Below are details of the target, its surroundings, defences and other data. It was from a much-improved Scampton that the 'Dambusters' of No 617 Squadron took off on the night of May 16th–17th 1943 for one of the most spectacular bombing raids of the war. /*Christopher Elliott collection.*

# Scampton
## Fliegerhorst

Länge (westl. Greenw.): 0°33′   Breite: 53°18′15″
Mißweisung: ~ 11°03′ (Mitte 1940) Zielhöhe über NN 65 m

Maßstab 1:10.560

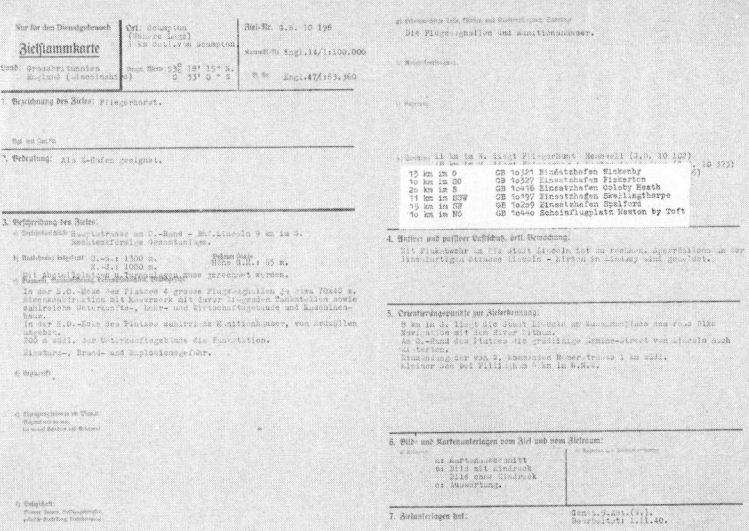

### GB 10 196  Fliegerhorst Scampton

| | | |
|---|---|---|
| 1) 4 Hallen | etwa | 16 000 qm |
| 2) 45 Unterkunftsgeb. | " | 8 000 qm |
| 3) 74 Munitionshäuser | " | 1 000 qm |
| 4) 74 Lehr-u. Wirtschaftsgeb. | " | 6 000 qm |
| 5) ansch. Funkstation | | 350 qm |
| 6) 4 Tankstellen | | |
| 7) 1 Kompensationsscheibe | | |
| 8) 1 Unterstand (Befehlsstelle?) | etwa | 500 qm |
| 9) Maschinenhaus | | 260 qm |
| 10) Flugleitung | | 350 qm |
| Bebaute Fläche | etwa | 32 460 qm |
| Gleisanschluß nicht vorhanden | | |

---

Nur für den Dienstgebrauch

**Zielstammkarte**

Verb. Grossbritannien
England (Abschnitt 14)

Ort: Scampton
(Nähere Lage)
16 km Nordl.v.Scampton

Ziel-Nr. G.B. 10 196

Massstab: Engl.14/1:100.000

" Engl.427/1:63.360

geogr.Breite 53°18′15″ n.Br.
0°33′ O v. Gr.

1. **Bezeichnung des Zieles:** Fliegerhorst.

2. **Bedeutung:** Als B-Hafen geeignet.

3. **Beschreibung des Zieles:**

4. **Unterer und seitlicher Luftschutz, örtl. Bewachung.**

5. **Orientierungspunkte zur Wiederkennung.**

6. **Bild- und Kartenunterlagen zum Ziel und zum Zielraum.**

7. **Zielunterlagen hef:**

Gnst.5.Abt.(K).
Bearbeitet: 1.11.40.

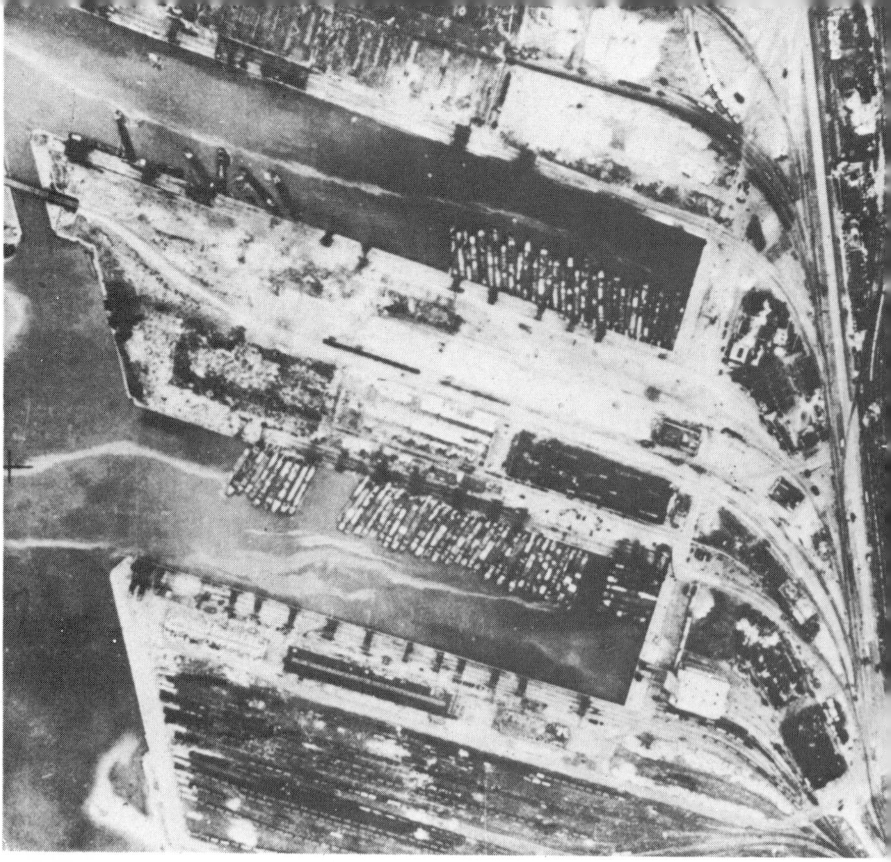

British reconnaissance photograph, taken in the summer of 1940, showing German invasion barges at Dunkirk. /*IWM.*

Reconnaissance cameras being taken out to a waiting F–8 Mosquito of the USAAF.

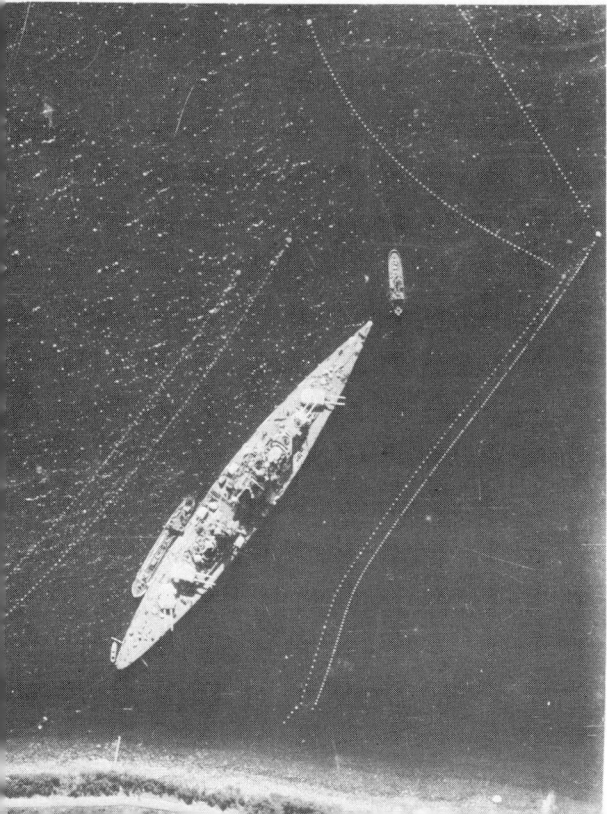

(Above) This photograph of the airfield at Peenemunde showed not only two Me 163 tailless rocket-powered fighters (near small building in centre) but scorch-marks on the airfield caused by their engines.

(Left) Tempting target: the German battleship *Tirpitz*, surrounded by torpedo nets, in Bogen Fjord, Narvik, July 1942.

(Top) Halifax B.III of No 171 Squadron, an RCM unit of 100 Group. Note additional aerials under nose and rear fuselage, and 'Window' chutes under fuselage. /P. J. R. Moyes

(Centre) Packed with electronic devices, a 100 Group Mosquito intruder sets out to hunt its prey in enemy skies. /IWM

(Bottom) Strange bulges, housing jamming devices, made the Fortresses of 100 Group different from those which spearheaded the USAAF's daylight bombing offensive. /IWM

(Top) Messerschmitt Me 262A–1a used for the first trials of *Lichtenstein SN–2* night-interception radar on a jet fighter.

(Centre) Opportunity for the RAF to examine *Flensburg* and *Lichtenstein SN–2* came when a German pilot landed his Ju 88G–1 by mistake at Woodbridge, Essex. /*IWM*

(Bottom) Following the successful testing of H$_2$S radar in this Mosquito, the aircraft of 139 Squadron were fitted with a special nose-mounted version and acted as Pathfinders for the Light Night Striking Force.

Early ECM: 'Window' falling from Lancasters during the 1,000-bomber raid on Essen, March 11th 1945. /IWM

'Operation Corona': This photograph shows the 'ghost voice' microphone over which spoof messages were passed to enemy night fighters and the gramophone for voice jamming. /IWM

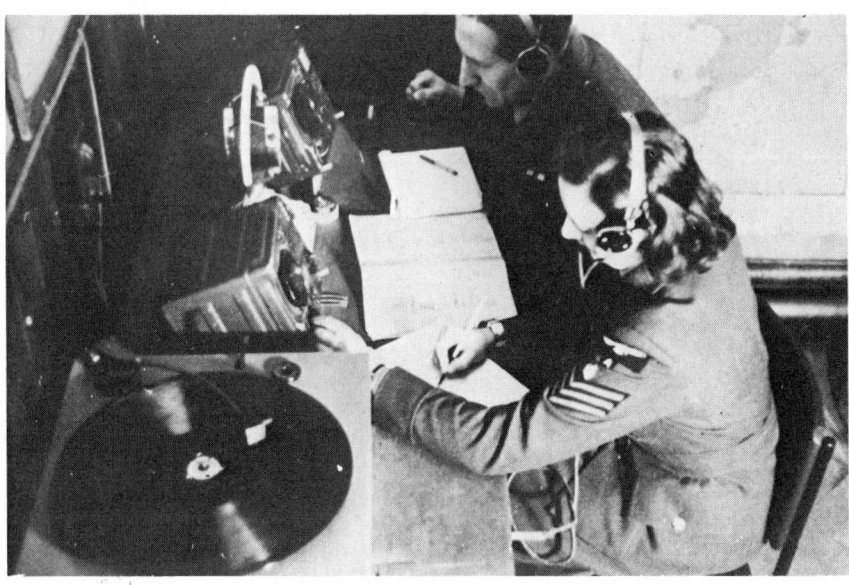

a big effort, with more than 700 aircraft in the attack force. The German radar controllers 'saw' many more than this. In fact, their screens were soon packed with so many 'blips' that they could not believe their eyes. One startled controller gave up trying to direct fighters to individual targets with a despairing cry: "There are too many hostiles." Another could only offer the conclusion that: "The enemy are reproducing themselves". He was nearer to the truth than he realised.

For two years the RAF had known that it could jam any existing form of radar by dropping strips of metal foil from its aircraft. The length of the strips had to be calculated precisely to match the known frequency of the radar to be neutralised. After that the strips, code-named Window, would fill the radar screens with clutter among which the 'blips' from the bombers were indistinguishable.

The snag was that Window was equally effective against British radars. Consequently the RAF decided that it dare not use the device operationally until such time as Bomber Command's losses began to soar to an unacceptable degree or the enemy bomber force was so stretched by a war on several fronts that it could no longer mount a heavy and prolonged offensive against the UK, shielded by Window.

By that July night in 1943, it seemed certain that the potential saving in lives and aircraft far outweighed the risks. So, as the bomber crews flew towards Hamburg, they dumped overboard bundles of Window at predetermined times and places—to the utter confusion of the defences. Only twelve British aircraft were lost.

Goering was so angry at the sudden blinding of his *Würzburgs* that he sacked General Kammhuber on the spot, and replaced him with General Schmid. Losses in the RAF bomber force during raids on German targets fell by 40 per cent and the only way in which the enemy could now direct his night fighters was by broadcasting a general report on the progress of a bomber stream, leaving the *Luftwaffe* pilots to find their targets individually as best they could.

It was at this moment that the 'ghost controllers' of Operation Corona began their misleading work.

The 'radio war' now became hectic. Corona was rendered ineffective when the Germans began fitting FuG 16 VHF short-range radio in all their night fighters. But the TRE had anticipated such a move by evolving a VHF jammer code-named Airborne Cigar, or ABC. Lancasters of No 101 Squadron, fitted with this equipment, were scattered throughout the bomber stream in all night raids from the end of 1943. On board each aircraft, a German-speaking crew member swept through the 38–42 megacycle band used by FuG 16, until he picked up the voice of the enemy fighter controller. It was then a simple matter to tune his jammer so that it would blot out the controller's messages.

After that, for a time, the enemy night-fighter pilots were expected to become music-lovers. As they searched the night sky for targets, they had to listen to broadcasts from the forces' radio station. If the usual endless stream of dance music changed suddenly to jazz, they had to set course towards RAF bombers heading for Berlin. A waltz indicated that Munich was the target; church music signified Munster, and so on. It was hardly to be expected that Britain's highly efficient 'radio spies' would fail for long to grasp the significance of the musical code, and soon the enemy was robbed of his entertainment as well as his novel system of ground control when a high-power transmitter known as Dartboard completely swamped all the music.

Desperately, German electronic experts devised new equipment to restore the efficiency of their defences. From early 1944, the *Luftwaffe*'s night fighters were fitted with FuG 350 *Naxos Z*, which enabled them to pick up and home on emissions from the bombers' H₂S radar; and FuG 227 *Flensburg*, which homed on signals from the Monica tail-warning radars which told the bomber crews if anything was approaching them from astern. In answer, Bomber Command simply stopped using Monica and restricted the use of $H_2S$.

The new FuG 220 *Lichtenstein SN–2*, which superseded *Lichtenstein BC*, was far more worrying. Unaffected either by jamming or the standard type of Window on its frequency of 90 megacycles, it came into large-scale service at a period when the efficiency of the German defences reached a new peak. Ground radars had become less vulnerable to Window and *Naxos Z* and *Flensburg* had not yet been countered. The night-fighter force was also at maximum strength, with no fewer than 650 twin-engined aircraft in service.

On the night of February 19/20th 1944, Bomber Command lost 78 out of 816 aircraft that attacked Leipzig. A raid on Berlin by 810 bombers on March 24/25th cost another 72 aircraft. Six days later, the *Luftwaffe* achieved its greatest-ever success against the night offensive by destroying 94 of the 795 aircraft despatched against Nuremberg. Clearly, such a loss rate could not be endured for long.

It was obvious from the reduced number of Serrate contacts that the enemy had introduced a new form of AI radar that was proof against existing countermeasures; but what was it? All attempts to learn the answer failed until a USAAF fighter brought back blurred camera-gun photographs of a night fighter that it had shot up at an enemy airfield. Study of the aerial array on the nose of the enemy aircraft gave a first clue to the frequency on which the night fighter AI was now working. Then, on July 13th 1944, the pilot of a Junkers Ju 88G, patrolling at night over the North Sea, lost his bearings and landed at RAF Woodbridge, Suffolk, instead of in Holland. The secrets were revealed, as it was fitted with both *Lichtenstein SN–2* and a *Flensburg* homer.

The *Luftwaffe* night-fighter force had shot its bolt. A change in the length of the RAF"s Window reduced the effectiveness of *Lichtenstein SN–2*, except against individual aircraft on the edges of a bomber stream, or stragglers. Even this small bonus disappeared when the Mosquitoes of No 192 Squadron and Fortresses of Nos 214 and 233 Squadrons began operating

Piperack in November 1944—an electronic jammer that cluttered AI screens as effectively as the old Ground Grocer had done.

These RAF Squadrons belonged to an entirely new unit of the Royal Air Force, designated No 100 Group. Formed on November 8th 1943, its task was well summarised by its motto 'Confound and Destroy', for its twin roles were to jam the radio and radar used by *Luftwaffe* night fighters and to provide long-range fighter protection for the aircraft of Bomber Command.

Initially, No 100 Group was allocated twelve squadrons, equipped with six different types of aircraft. The Halifaxes of 171 Squadron, Stirlings of 199 Squadron, Fortresses of 214 Squadron and Liberators of 223 Squadron carried the radio and radar jamming devices. The Mosquitoes of 23, 85, 141, 157, 169, 239 and 515 Squadrons were the intruders who stalked the *Luftwaffe*'s night fighters, shooting down an average of three per night and making the rest of the enemy crews edgy and less efficient. Finally, there were the 'ferrets' of No 192 Squadron, whose mixed bag of Wellingtons, Halifaxes and Mosquitoes had the vital, unenviable task of probing the secrets of the enemy's electronic defence systems in hostile skies.

On any night, whether or not a major raid was planned, aircraft equipped with Mandrel would orbit carefully-selected spots outside enemy airspace to jam the German early-warning ground radars. Just eight aircraft, spaced at regular intervals, could blot out a 130-mile (210km) sector of the defensive cover.

Other aircraft from 100 Group were despatched on up to three feint attacks each night to protect the main bomber force. By dumping Window at a high rate, ten to twenty aircraft could produce the same effect on enemy radar as the much larger main force, using its Window at normal concentrations. Close-cover jamming for both the main and feint attacks was provided by aircraft fitted with Piperack and a device known as Jostle which produced a raucous warbling noise, rather like bagpipes, on the enemy fighter control frequencies.

Typical of the successes achieved by 100 Group was that of December 4th 1944, when Bomber Command attacked Hagen and Hamm at opposite ends of the Ruhr valley and Heilbronn and Karlsruhe in southern Germany. By laying a trail of Window towards the heart of the Ruhr and then dropping spoof target markers, the aircraft of 100 Group were able to attract nearly 100 night fighters away from the main bomber fleets, and only fifteen RAF aircraft were lost from a total of 892 involved in the night's operations.

Goering blamed such statistics on the incompetence of the German ground controllers, claiming that he never had any difficulty in distinguishing between real and feint attacks. Had he passed on the secret of his second sight to General Schmid the *Luftwaffe* would have been saved considerable heartache. As it was, morale slumped lower and lower.

On the night of December 6th 1944, in a typical action by a Mosquito of 85 Squadron, a single one-second burst of fire was sufficient to kill

Hauptmann Hans-Heinz Augenstein, an Me 110 night fighter ace who had claimed 46 victories. One of his colleagues, Hauptmann Hans Krause, survived with a score of 28 victories only because he always approached his base in a dive from 10,000ft (3,000m) and then landed quickly on an unlit, or semi-lit, strip. Other pilots, trying the same technique, lacked his skill or luck and ended up in blazing wreckage on the ground or on hillsides.

At a conference in the Berlin Air Ministry on January 5th 1945, General Adolf Galland, commander of the *Luftwaffe* fighter force, is reported to have said: "To-day the night fighter achieves nothing. The reason for this lies in the enemy's jamming operations, which completely blot out ground and airborne search equipment. All other reasons are secondary."

So was born the new military science of electronic countermeasures (ECM), a 20th century partner for older forms of reconnaissance that played a still-unappreciated part in ensuring Allied victory in 1945.

# 6 Open Skies

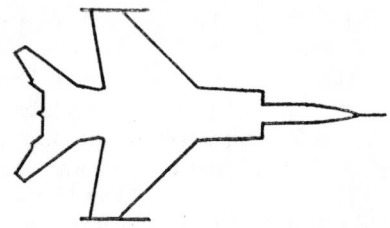

Sixty-eight, sixty-nine, seventy . . . his mind automatically counted the paces as he neared the end of his westward beat. Hong Kil-Dong came to a halt, lowered the butt of his rifle to the ground and leaned the barrel against his chest, thus freeing his hands which he chafed together in an attempt to kindle a little warmth into them. He stamped his feet, for the same reason, and wondered why it always seemed so bitterly cold just before dawn.

A faint breeze, another harbinger of the new day, rustled the leaves as a first trace of pearly light began to lift the shutter of night.

Hong shivered, shouldered his rifle and turned to begin his trudge eastwards, glancing every few seconds to his left. He wanted to be certain, as soon as there was enough light to see, that the gentle slope upwards from the border held no enemy. Not that he expected to see one; but during the last few weeks there had been some border incidents, occasional exchanges of rifle fire, and one couldn't be too careful.

A new sound came from the north. It worried Hong, for he couldn't understand what it was. Almost like the clatter of distant tanks. He laughed quietly to himself: the day was yet to dawn when Hong Kil-Dong would see such monsters in the land of his birth.

Sixty-nine, seventy. . . . He halted again as he reached the other end of his beat and tried, once more, to coax a little warmth into his hands and feet. He turned to retrace his steps, this time glancing to his right.

All was quiet. But now it was light enough to see darker masses of . . . of what? . . . that seemed to move and then, suddenly, did move. Hong knew the enemy was close at hand.

He started to run to the guard post, but before he could reach its flimsy shelter or raise the alarm, a shattering burst of fire from an automatic weapon had ended all of Hong's worldly worries. As he went to meet his ancestors the strange sound roared again in his senses—the thunder of tanks. He never did see them. . . .

As Hong's blood stained the earth the colour of the rising sun, similar events were taking place all along the 38th Parallel. It was 04.00 hours on June 25th 1950. The North Korean infantry, spearheaded by Soviet-built tanks, streamed across the border in their thousands to attack the Republic of Korea.

Almost thirty-two years earlier had come the end of the 'war to end wars'. So unrealistic was the subsequent partition of Europe, so ineffective the controlling power of the League of Nations that, just twenty-one years later, Europe had been at war again.

By the time World War II ended officially, with Japanese signature of the formal instrument of surrender on board the USS *Missouri* on September 2nd 1945, it seemed reasonable to assume that world governments might have acquired sufficient wisdom to ensure lasting peace. There was, too, a new and then-unique reason why any country was unlikely to make a major aggressive move: the United States held exclusively a 'big stick', in the form of the atomic bomb.

We should know better than to expect perfection from an imperfect world.

Soldiers of East and West had joined hands in greeting amidst the dust and smoke of conflict that, in the closing stages of the battle for Berlin, had raged down internationally-known 'strasses'. Now all was quiet. There remained the stench of war; the rubble-strewn roads; and hunger. It was symbolic, said the optimists. From this misery of death and destruction, that had once been Hitler's Third Reich, would come at last a Europe united as never before.

Perhaps it would be unkind to comment that, in one sense, the last four words were horrifyingly prophetic. Wisps of smoke still pinpointed long-smouldering wreckage; rubble littered streets that might have been those of a ghost town; and none of Berlin's hungry survivors had eaten a decent meal before the Eastern 'comrades' retreated behind the icy barrier known as Communism.

With the end of war in Europe, the RAF was reduced to a fraction of its peak wartime strength and, with VJ-Day behind them, the citizens of America demanded their menfolk back home from the farthest reaches of the Pacific. Within four months the 2¼ million strong USAAF had dwindled to less than a million: by May 1947 it had shrunk further to a mere 303,000 men.

Behind their 'Iron Curtain', the Communists watched the world situation with growing interest: there was much to give them thought.

Great Britain had already made a maximum contribution to the restoration of peace in Europe. She was no longer in a position to re-occupy her traditional role of international peace-keeper.

During the 18 months which followed VJ-Day, the Americans were busy withdrawing from military responsibility around the world, leaving only policing forces in Germany, Japan and a few other vital outposts. US military forces had been run down to a minimum.

The overall result was that in many areas of the Far East conditions were ripe for Communist expansion, and the watchers in the Kremlin were not slow to move.

Thus, by 1947, military and political leaders in the West were aware of a rapidly expanding and highly dangerous situation; one which was grave because there was virtually no communication of any value with the Eastern bloc. An impasse had arisen, giving birth to the now well-known term 'Cold War'.

By mid-1948 the Communists considered that the moment had come to test the depth of Western solidarity. On the night of June 24th 1948, Allied occupying forces in West Berlin received a teletype message from the Russian zone: '. . . the Soviet Military Administration is compelled to halt all passenger and freight traffic to and from Berlin to-morrow at 06.00 hours because of technical difficulties. . . .'

To make clear the significance of this move, it must be appreciated that Berlin had become virtually an island within Germany, surrounded by the Russian zone. This meant that the Communists controlled all surface routes to the city. Deny access, they argued, and there was a good chance that the Allied occupation forces would withdraw, leaving the whole of Berlin under the thumb of the Kremlin.

The fuse of a third World War had been lit. Could the West stamp it out in time? Fortunately, they had free access to the capital via three air corridors: by these routes the citizens and occupying military forces were sustained with food, fuel and all other essential supplies for a period of ten months. From this operation, which became known as the Berlin Airlift, the Communists received a loud and clear message: no matter what the cost, the Western world was determined to maintain peace.

Peace reigned; an uneasy, worrying sort of peace. Worrying because it was known that the Soviets were still spending huge sums of money on military expansion. It was reported, for example, that during 1948 the Soviets had built twelve military aircraft for every one produced in the United States. How long could it be before some new move would threaten a peace that, however uneasy, was infinitely preferable to a shooting war? It seemed that it would not be long delayed.

This, then, was the situation until the day that Hong Kil-Dong joined his ancestors. The initial attack was extremely violent and had the advantage of surprise. The UN Security Council met at once and asked that all member nations should help to enforce the North Koreans to withdraw behind the 38th Parallel. Thus, troops of many countries fought in Korea under the United Nations banner, but the war in the air was largely the province of the USAF, USN and RAAF.

People associated with aviation will tell you that this three-year war saw the coming-of-age of the helicopter as a combat aircraft. Not so well known is that it signalled a re-birth of aerial reconnaissance.

Demands upon national military budgets had left nothing for the development of specialised reconnaissance aircraft or techniques for years; this meant that the state-of-the-art was very much the same as it had been on VJ-Day. To make matters worse, little apparent need for military photo-reconnaissance meant that the all-essential system of administration that put the right photographs on the right desk at the right time had grown cobwebs.

With the outbreak of war in Korea, UN forces discovered very quickly that their need for aerial reconnaissance was even more vital than it had been in the closing stages of World War II. Not only was it more vital—a much greater number of reconnaissance sorties was necessary. They found out, equally quickly, that the existing PR units were quite unable to meet the demands.

The reasons were not hard to find. The conflict in Korea was of a 'limited' nature, with political and military considerations of almost equal importance. For fear of diplomatic consequences it was essential that many otherwise-attractive military targets should be avoided. Only adequate PR could ensure that UN forces generally were made aware of forbidden targets and, at the same time, could provide evidence—when necessary—that no aggressive action had been initiated against any particular building or area. Furthermore, the particular nature of the terrain favoured the attackers: detailed and massive reconnaissance was necessary to find the North Korean or Chinese needles in the jungle haystacks.

There was an even more important factor. The forbidden targets included Manchurian airfields at the other side of the Yalu River. Regular reconnaissance of these airfields could provide important information, such as a build-up of fighters or transports, signifying potential attacks of different kinds; or the introduction of new aircraft types or equipment. It would even be possible, by discovering the length of runway needed for take-off by the new Russian-built MiG–15 jet-fighters, to learn much about their capabilities.

Thus the requirement. Acquisition of the right photographs was a different problem. For the first time reconnaissance sorties were being made by jet aircraft, using cameras and equipment developed for slower-flying piston-engined machines. Shots made at jet-speed suffered from blur and were of little use. If the 'plane slowed sufficiently to ensure sharp, detailed pictures, it became a sitting duck for the MiGs.

The most hazardous sorties took place in the area known as MiG Alley, to the west of the Chongchon River. Usual procedure was for a single jet-powered recce aircraft to penetrate the area at around 19,000ft (5,800m) with a high-altitude cover of F–86 Sabres. The recce pilot had a difficult job, searching for troop concentrations, bridges and landing strips, avoiding enemy flak and keeping an ever-watchful eye for the MiGs that could come streaking down to attack with a murderous burst of cannon fire. If he spotted the MiGs in time he gave his engine the gun, diving like a rocket to ground level and banking steeply to get back over the line in a bucking and twisting terrain-hugging flight, leaving the MiGs and Sabres to fight it out.

As the intensity of the battle grew, reconnaissance by night became of particular importance, for the North Koreans soon realised that it was far safer to move under cover of darkness. This increased the problems, for the means of providing adequate illumination for night photography had not been developed. Even when the illumination problem was resolved, the cameras then available were unable to record sufficient detail under night conditions: not until after the Korean War was the ideal camera produced.

Some alternative solution had to be found. The most simple proved the most effective—a return to the wartime technique of visual observation. The observer for a particular mission would spend several hours in complete darkness. When the time came to go aboard his aircraft his eyes were protected from any chance sight of light, and not until the aircraft was over its area of operation did he remove the goggles that shaded his eyes. Lying in a prone position, in a completely dark section of the nose, he was then able to see, with surprising detail, much of the scene below. Even when close detail was denied, it was often possible to provide the operational centre with information that was worth following up.

The limited endurance of the new fuel-hungry jet fighter-bombers brought introduction of an operational technique known as 'Circle 10' missions. Night sightings of enemy movement, however brief, were reported to the operational centre. At first light this centre would despatch piston-engined reconnaissance aircraft to search a circle of ten miles (16km) diameter around the point of suspect. If any tell-tale sign of the enemy was found the recce aircraft would call in the fighter-bombers, which proceeded to saturate the area with rockets, bombs or napalm, the latter proving particularly effective in heavily wooded positions.

An extension of this reconnaissance activity came with the introduction of tactical air co-ordinators. A pilot and observer, accommodated in a modified T–6 (Harvard) trainer aircraft, maintained visual reconnaissance in battle areas. It was no enviable task. Extra equipment needed for the new role meant that the trainers were far from manoeuvrable and that their effective ceiling brought them within easy range of enemy anti-aircraft fire.

Twisting and turning, diving and climbing to avoid the flak, looking over their shoulders for enemy fighters, and at the same time trying to concentrate on the battle being fought below them, this was no occupation for aircrew whose principal concern was longevity. Over the battlefield for up to three hours at a time, they faced survival odds that would make any self-respecting insurance broker find a new way of life.

The value of this kind of reconnaissance was enormous. On-the-spot appreciation of the fighting below, relayed by radio to an operations centre, enabled senior command to react to an adverse situation almost before it happened. Not only could the two-man team supply a running commentary; they were in a position to call in an air strike when it was most needed, and were equipped to mark the target with phosphorous rockets. Little wonder that the North Koreans reserved an especial hatred for these little 'planes and made every possible effort to claw them out of the sky. As one might expect, their losses were heavy. But the concept was proven, especially for this particular kind of limited warfare, and it was soon planned to develop a new kind of aircraft to fill this vital reconnaissance role.

The Korean War saw the introduction of another, revolutionary reconnaissance technique that has strengthened enormously the scope of the photographic eye in the sky.

For a long time efforts had been made to develop a special colour film to facilitate the detection of camouflaged objects. It was known that infra-red film stock could be valuable for this particular task, but its exposure rating was slow and it was necessary also to combat haze.

The Aerial Kodacolor film that emerged during the Korean War was a complex film stock to provide high speed and haze elimination, with an infra-red coating and filter to record in red all natural vegetation embodying chlorophyll, and a panchromatic emulsion and filter to capture a green image of non-chlorophyll-containing objects. It doesn't sound very exciting but the results are dramatic. A photograph of a field containing, for example, a tank, depicts the field in red and the tank in green. The latter sticks out like a sore thumb.

But that is not all. Try and camouflage the tank to prevent its detection. Camouflage net? No good—man-made. Tree branches? No good—they die quickly and the chlorophyll no longer gives a red image on the film. And if the tank was driven into the field recently the grass that it crushed is also dead, and leaves clearly defined tell-tale tracks.

Now you can see the importance of this film, and appreciate how vital it was in Korea. It is no exaggeration to claim for it the major proportion of detections of enemy positions and equipment, however well concealed, following its introduction.

Stereoscopic and panoramic cameras were not new, of course, but one operation which depended upon their use is of special interest.

It was planned to make an amphibious landing behind the North Korean lines late in 1950. The most suitable site was at Inchon, the port serving the city of Seoul, but it had one major drawback, namely a very wide variation of water level between low and high tide. So wide a variation, in fact, that US Navy officers considered the operation too hazardous to undertake. They had not taken into account the scope of aerial reconnaissance and skilled photographic interpretation.

While the Navy made their preparations for the landings, reconnaissance aircraft set about the task of gaining information that could enable the photographic interpreters to predict a date and time when the tide height would be adequate to permit landing craft to put the Marines ashore.

Skimming the wave tops, the reconnaissance jets thundered up to the port of Inchon day after day, photographing the sea walls at every stage of the tide, and at precise times. When the interpreters studied the resulting stereo photos they were able to predict, with remarkable accuracy, an optimum date and time for the landing: 17.30 hours, September 15th.

However doubtful the Navy might have been, the operation was mounted with traditional courage and expertise. To their amazement, the tide height was within inches of the predicted figure and the landings were made easily. Within days Seoul was captured.

Not until July 27th 1953, was peace restored in Korea, but there was no doubt of the valuable contribution that aerial reconnaissance had played in the three-year war that ended without victory for either side.

The post-mortem that followed left little doubt in the minds of UN leaders that the main reason for this Communist-inspired invasion was Soviet belief that the Western powers had run down their forces to such a level that they would never dare to become involved in a shooting war.

It was clear to both East and West that, in an age when diplomatic negotiations were incapable of maintaining peace, the only alternative was the establishment of striking forces so potent in their capability that neither side would be prepared to risk any major military action for fear of annihilating retaliation.

At the end of World War II only the United States had such a capability, but Russia had detonated its first atomic bomb in 1949, and America's 'big stick' was no longer a monopoly. It was a forlorn hope that the United Nations could do anything to control the production or use of atomic weapons and the US was aware that it could no longer, as in 1919, maintain an isolated indifference to world affairs. Thus, it began development of a thermonuclear (hydrogen) bomb. The nuclear arms race was initiated; the age of the deterrent powers had come.

There were other aspects of this situation that caused the US leaders considerable concern. For example, they did not know whether any other nation possessed nuclear weapons and might be prepared to use them in a clandestine manner to seek world domination. Science fiction writers had already dreamed up many ways in which master criminals or rogue governments might hold the world to ransom. And science fiction writers had often made surprisingly accurate predictions of things to come.

There was another nagging thought. Was it possible that another nation might already possess new and terrifying weapons of which American intelligence had no knowledge?

It was against this background that the American President, Dwight D. Eisenhower, proposed at a Summit Conference in Geneva, in July 1955, a new and revolutionary approach to the problem, to 'ease the fears of war in the anxious hearts of people everywhere'. This was no diplomat's tongue-in-the-cheek statement. The fears were real. Ex-servicemen of all nations, relegated to the reserve after service in World War II, had dreaded the postman's knock during the Korean War, for fear they might be recalled to active service. Women throughout the world were afraid to have children in an age when an unstable individual could initiate an unthinking act of aggression that would, in turn, start a chain-reaction of events leading to atomic war and a possible end of civilisation as we know it. Anxious hearts, indeed.

In his speech to the Conference, the American President addressed himself principally to the delegates of the Soviet Union. "I propose, therefore," he said, "that we take a practical step, that we begin an arrangement, very quickly, as between ourselves — immediately." These steps would include:

"To give to each other a complete blueprint of our military establishments, from beginning to end, from one end of our countries to the other; lay out the establishments and provide the blueprints to each other."

"Next, to provide within our countries facilities for aerial photography to the other country—we to provide you the facilities within our country, ample facilities for aerial reconnaissance, where you can make all the pictures you choose and take them to your country to study. You to provide exactly the same facilities for us and we to make these examinations, and by this step to convince the world that we are providing as between ourselves against the possibility of great surprise attack, thus lessening danger and relaxing tension. . . ."

In simple terms, this Open Skies proposal was for a mutual photographic reconnaissance policy. How could such a move be effective in preventing military aggression? How could it reduce world tension? Would it work? A lot of questions and no clear-cut answers. Not then. Only now are we beginning to appreciate the vision of Eisenhower's plan.

As we have already seen, the war in Korea had improved immeasurably the status and scope of aerial reconnaissance. But how, you may argue, can battlefield surveillance techniques lead to any lessening of tension between countries that have a mutual distrust of each other?

To understand the potential of Eisenhower's plan, it is essential to know the capability of aerial reconnaissance at that time. As a first point, what was the capability of a typical recce aircraft of that period?

Let us look, for example, at the USAF's RB–47 medium reconnaissance aircraft, developed from the advanced and highly successful swept-wing six-turbojet Boeing B–47 Stratojet bomber. Specially modified for the reconnaissance role, it could carry as many as seven precision cameras, each able to operate automatically and continuously to record without break the ground beneath the aircraft's track. It was possible for the RB–47, flying at a height of 40,000ft (12,200m), to photograph a million square miles (2,590,000km²) of territory in one three-hour flight. In a single east–west overflight of the US, a continuous strip some 490 miles (789km) wide and 2,700 miles (4,345km) in length could be recorded in less than four hours.

To enhance the scope of the RB–47 it had flight refuelling capability, which could give round-the-world range if needed.

One may wonder what useful information can be gleaned from a photograph taken at nearly eight miles (13km) above the Earth's surface. This is where the skill of the photographic interpreter comes into play. Perhaps the section of photograph which he is examining includes an enemy airfield. Knowing the altitude from which the shot was taken, and the focal length of the camera lens, he can measure—to within a few feet—the dimensions of the runways, hangars and other installations. From his specialised knowledge he can tell what type of aircraft could use such a runway and make an intelligent estimate of the operational capabilities of such an airfield. He can tell how many aircraft it might handle, and can often predict its fuel storage capacity. This can be achieved without any other information, even without sight of a single aircraft on the airfield.

From a low-level photograph, which is called for if an initial interpretation shows inexplicable factors that require further investigation, he can learn even more. One photograph of an airfield, taken by an aircraft flying at 525mph (845km/h) at a height of 60ft (18m), showed an aircraft being serviced on the tarmac. Despite the high speed and low altitude, an enlargement of the aircraft's wing was so clear that it was possible to count the rivets on its upper surface. One can imagine what other technical detail is visible to the skilled interpreter.

Interpretation is not, of course, limited to military installations. Specialists in particular fields can estimate the potential of industrial plant. A photograph of a steel mill, for example, would enable an expert on steel production to determine the type of mill, the product it manufactures and its production capacity.

A shot of city streets, taken by an aircraft flying so high that it is invisible from the ground, would provide detailed information on income groups of a particular area, the availability of water, sewage, electric and telephone services. On occasion it has been possible to determine whether a house occupant has mowed his lawn by conventional mower or rotary scythe.

Day or night reconnaissance makes little difference, for newly-developed cameras and flash-bombs of more than four billion candle-power, produce pictures by night that lack only daylight shadow to aid height estimation.

Regular inspection of a particular area allows comparison; and expanding installations, new buildings, roads, and services all have a tale to tell. An established airfield, of only minor interest, is worthy of closer study if a random shot shows that its runways are being lengthened or new barrack blocks being built.

From the foregoing it is apparent how much could be achieved by an Open Skies policy. No longer would a nation be unaware of military preparations by a potential enemy. If the reaction was to make counter-preparations to meet any attack then, by mutual aerial inspection, this knowledge would be available to the enemy who would know that the effort was not worthwhile.

This was the far-sighted prospect of Eisenhower's plan. He knew, though, that the Soviet Union was unlikely to accept his proposals in full. Instead, he attempted to gain partial acceptance by proposing an interim step, in which a fairly large area of each country—each containing a port, an airfield, a rail terminal and a non-secret military installation—would come under regular surveillance from the other side. From this method of test inspection would come many valuable lessons and it would, at the same time, help to build mutual confidence.

The time was not ripe. Despite worldwide publicity for the plan, which was considered generally as being a move in the right direction and one which must relieve world tension, the Soviets were not prepared to share with anyone information regarding their build-up of nuclear power.

On August 4th 1955, Marshal Bulganin referred to the proposal in a speech to the Supreme Soviet:

"The real effectiveness of such measures would not be great", he said. "During unofficial talks with leaders of the United States government, we straight-forwardly declared that aerial photography cannot give the expected results, because both countries stretch over vast territories in which, if one desired, one could conceal anything.

"One must also take into consideration the fact that the proposed plan touches only the territories belonging to the two countries, leaving out the armed forces and military installations situated in the territories of other states."

The Russian attitude had been predictable. Which meant that new measures had to be found to gain, for the Western world, accurate information on Soviet weapons and intentions.

The new measures had already been initiated. In December 1954 approval had been given for development of a revolutionary new reconnaissance aircraft that would be able to learn many of the Soviet Union's secrets. Designed by Kelly Johnson of Lockheed, it had been taking shape in a top-secret hangar known as the 'Skunk Works' at Lockheed's Burbank plant.

The first successful test flight of the new aircraft—known as the U–2—took place very shortly after Bulganin's rejection of the Open Skies plan. Little did he know that the Soviet skies would soon be wide open to this amazing aircraft!

# 7 U-2 Story

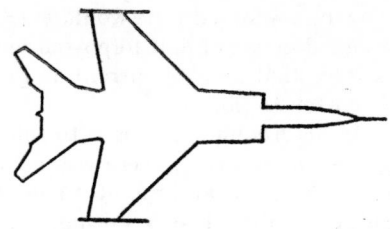

A sudden blare of klaxon horns shattered the peace of a quiet Spring morning: their anguished notes rose and fell with an all-demanding urgency as if they would waken the dead. The Russian anti-aircraft crew, for whom the alarm was intended, doubled to action stations. Like servicemen of any nation, their minds and tongues posed dozens of questions for which they were unlikely to receive an answer. "What's the panic?", "What's the target?", "Another false alarm?" and, most difficult of all, "Where's the target?" Unspoken or half-phrased questions were still-born as sharp commands urged them to prepare their shrouded missiles for firing.

Of the target there was no sign at all. No pinpoint shape pencilled a warning contrail across the blue sky. Only the glowing tubes of a radar installation had a story to tell: of an alien aircraft, silent and invisible, riding precariously the thinning atmosphere some 13 miles (21km) above.

In answer to the commands of radar and integrated computer the missile launchers came to life, inching around, changing their elevation, as if guided by invisible hands. Another imperative alarm warned of the beginning of the firing sequence, an ear-piercing din that was lost quickly in the thunder of noise that marked ignition. The missile, poised for a moment on a pillar of flame and smoke, accelerated into the sky with a hollow roar of sound that numbed the brain. . . .

At that same instant of time, the pilot of the high-flying reconnaissance aircraft was enjoying the security and solitude of height, busy with the task of controlling his aircraft, ensuring that he was maintaining course and altitude.

Suddenly, without warning, he sensed rather than felt the shock of an explosion. As his aircraft bucked he flicked his eyes from instruments to sky. He was surrounded by a glow of orange light and, almost immediately, the nose of the aircraft pitched down into a steep dive. He realised that the moment had come when he must fight for his life, his machine in an uncontrollable spin. By the time he managed to escape from the doomed aircraft he had dropped some 40,000ft (12,200m) towards the ground.

Then it was quiet and cold. He was dazed by the speed of events and his exertions to escape. Only minutes before he had been cocooned in the security of routine, thinking of his boyhood home in far away Kentucky.

Now he wondered if he would ever see America again. His mind raced with a kaleidoscope of half-forgotten incidents, among which was one repetitive pattern that seemed current and urgent . . . his parachute ripcord: he had forgotten to pull it.

As his reeling brain tried to command a lethargic hand to reach out and grasp the pull-ring, there was a sudden sharp jerk. A barometric control, set to operate at around 15,000ft (4,600m), had opened the parachute automatically. The billowing orange and white canopy above his head brought a sense of ease.

Now he was floating down serenely, to a landscape that could easily have been part of an American scene. There were gentle hills, wooded slopes, a lake, farms and a village. Too soon the ground was racing up to meet him, and he made a heavy landing that almost knocked him senseless.

He came back to reality as he was helped to his feet by a farm labourer, and could see men, women and children running towards him, to see for themselves this strange visitor from the sky.

The day was May 1st 1960. The American, Francis Gary Powers, had landed in the Soviet Union.

Within hours, he was secure in Lubyanka Prison, Moscow, headquarters of the KGB. Within days, news of his capture was flashed around the world, creating a train of international repercussions. The important Summit meeting scheduled to take place in Paris on May 16th was cancelled: President Eisenhower's invitation to visit Russia in June was withdrawn. The slightly reduced tension that had begun to ease relations between East and West was destroyed overnight, and the United States was placed temporarily in a most embarrassing situation.

The natural and inevitable question is 'Was it worth the cost?' To find the answer we must go back in time almost five-and-a-half years, to December 1954, when the USAF had given approval for development of the U–2.

It will be recalled that, at the time, despite most strenuous efforts from the West, the leaders of the Soviet Union were not inclined to co-operate in any mutual policy of disarmament.

It was in this period of mounting tension that the American President had evolved his Open Skies proposal. Also at about the same time, C. L. ('Kelly') Johnson, chief designer of the American Lockheed Company, had drawn up plans for a revolutionary new reconnaissance aircraft that would enable his country to acquire vital photographic intelligence without political or human risk. The availability of such information would at least give the West some warning of moves taking place behind the Iron Curtain.

For the new aircraft to gain such information, it needed to be entirely different from anything that had ever been created. It needed, for example, to fly so high that the chance of intercepting it was almost nil. Another requirement was long range, to permit overflight of the vast territory of the Soviet Union.

(Above) Factory at Deutz on the east bank of the Rhine before and after the 1,000-bomber raid on Cologne in May 1942. Such reconnaissance coverage of targets was essential to ensure that the bomber offensive was used effectively.

(Left) Some of the 800 craters left by RAF Bomber Command at Volkel airfield, Holland, on September 3rd 1944. /IWM

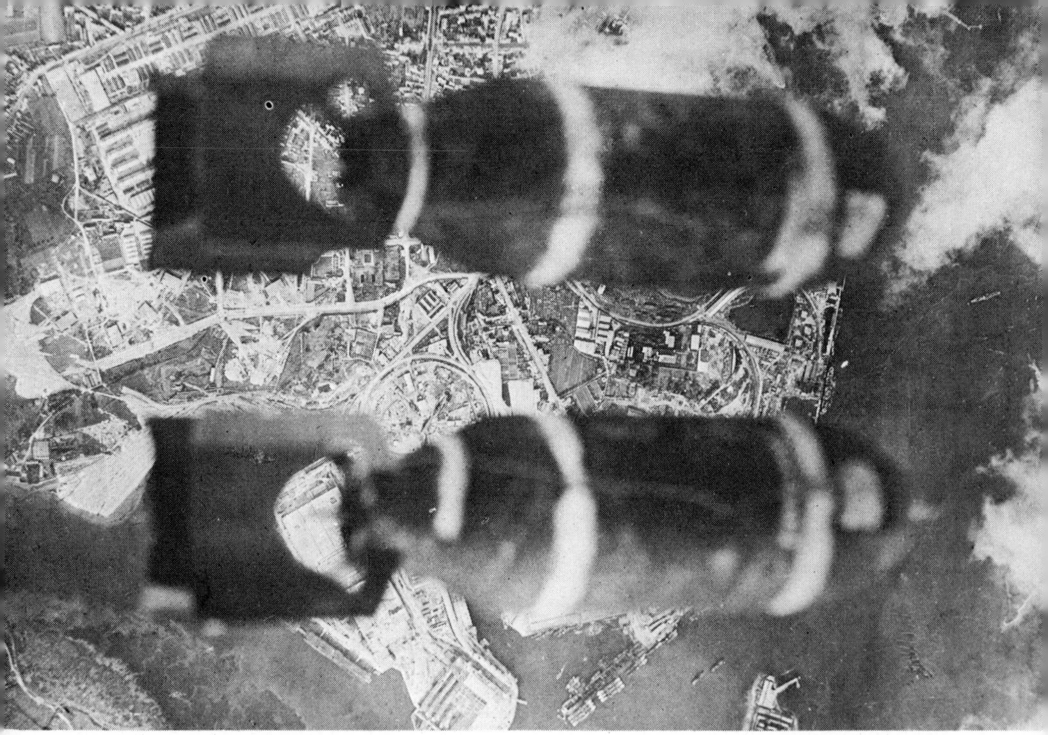

Photographs of this kind, taken at the moment of bomb release, provided confirmation that crews had attacked the right target.

The results of an attack were often recorded by dramatic photographs obtained in low-level 'dicing' sorties. This main line railway viaduct at Bielefeld had been pounded by the Lancasters of 617 Squadron, using 22,000lb and 12,000lb bombs. /IWM

(top) Other targets for 12,000lb bombs dropped by the 'Dambusters' of 617 Squadron
included a mysterious V-weapon installation at Wizernes, in the Pas de Calais. Item 1 in
this subsequent Mosquito photograph shows a huge concrete dome over the underground
workings; 2 is a hammerhead crane; 3 a completed concrete blockhouse and 4 another
concrete building.

(above) First air force to operate jet reconnaissance aircraft was the wartime *Luftwaffe*.
The single-seat 461mph Arado Ar 234Bs even eluded Britain's air defences during sorties
the autumn of 1944.

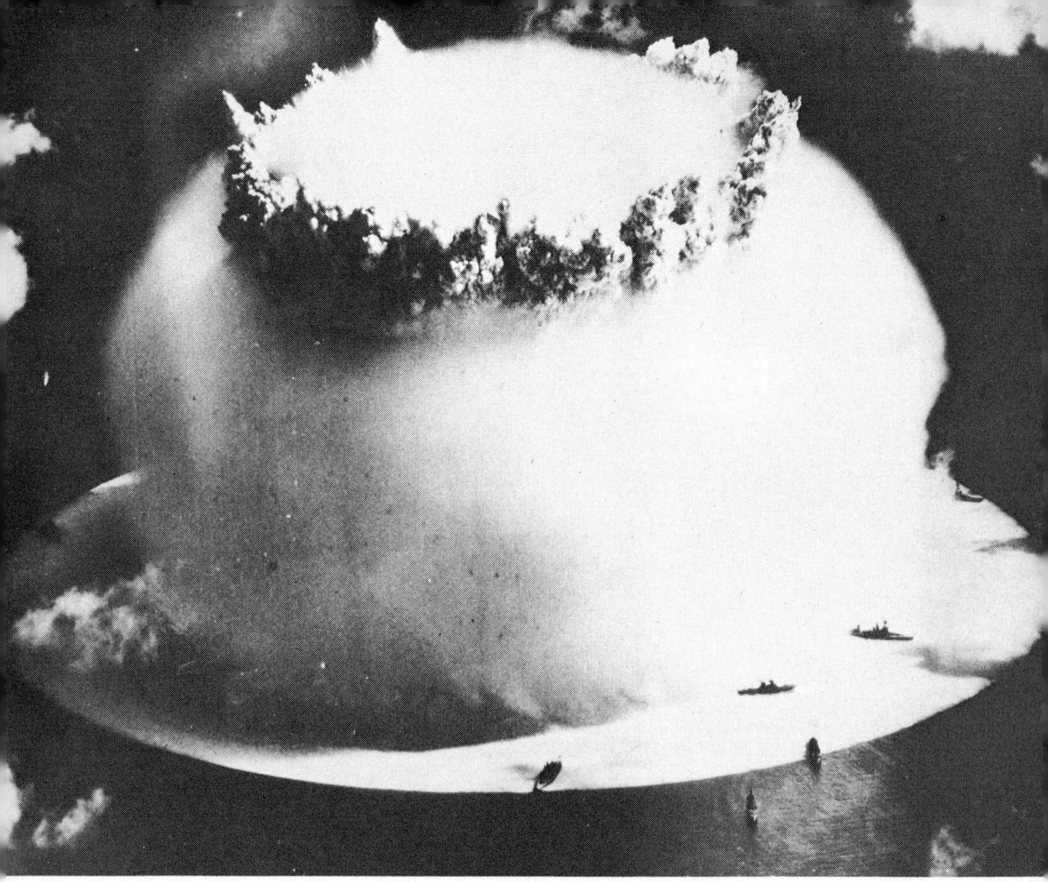

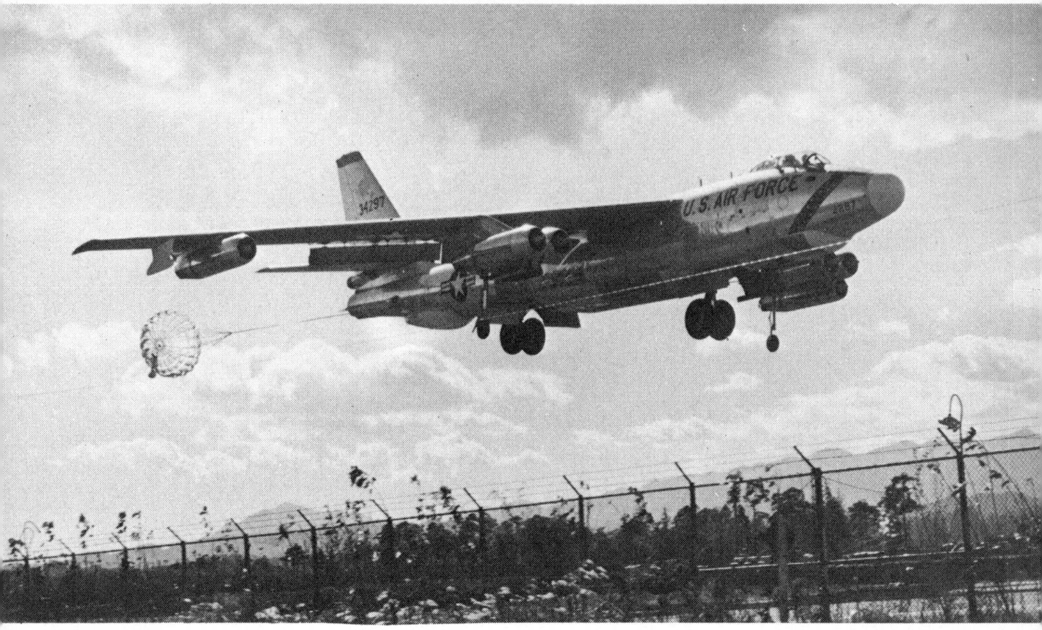
34297
U.S. AIR FORCE

(Above) The big eight-jet Boeing Stratofortress also had its special reconnaissance versions. This pressurised capsule being hoisted into the bomb-bay of an RB–52B carried two men and cameras or electronic countermeasures (ECM) equipment.

(Top left) Nuclear explosion at Bikini Atoll. Such post-war tests, added to the frightful wartime death and destruction at Hiroshima and Nagasaki, left no doubt of what might be the fate of mankind if the nuclear deterrent policy failed.

(Left) The USAF's Boeing B–47 Stratojet was a spearhead of America's nuclear striking force. Little-publicised variants included the RB–47H, which carried three extra men and special equipment in its bomb-bay to detect and locate surface radar stations operated by 'the other side'. /T. Matsuzaki

ЛЕТЧИК СБИТОГО САМОЛЕТА США
ФРЕНСИС ГАРРИ ПАУЭРС

POWERS FRANCIS GARY, THE PILOT OF THE SHOT AMERICAN PLANE

Е ДОКУМЕНТЫ
РАФИИ ПАУЭРСА

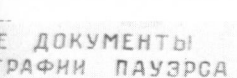

(Above) A U–2 touching down after flight. Having jettisoned its underwing 'balancers' after take-off, the pilot had to keep the wings level as long as possible as the aircraft lost speed, to reduce damage to the unprotected wingtips. /*Robert Archer*

(Below) Despite the Powers incident, use of the U–2 was completely vindicated when aircraft of this type discovered Soviet plans to install missiles in Cuba in 1962. Confirmation was obtained by RF–8A Crusaders in daring low-level photographic missions from a US Navy carrier.

(Top left) Aftermath of the notorious U–2 'spy-plane' incident of May Day 1960: photographs of pilot Gary Powers at an exhibition in Moscow's Gorky Park of Rest and Culture.

(Left) Photographs, certificates and other personal possessions found on Powers after his capture.

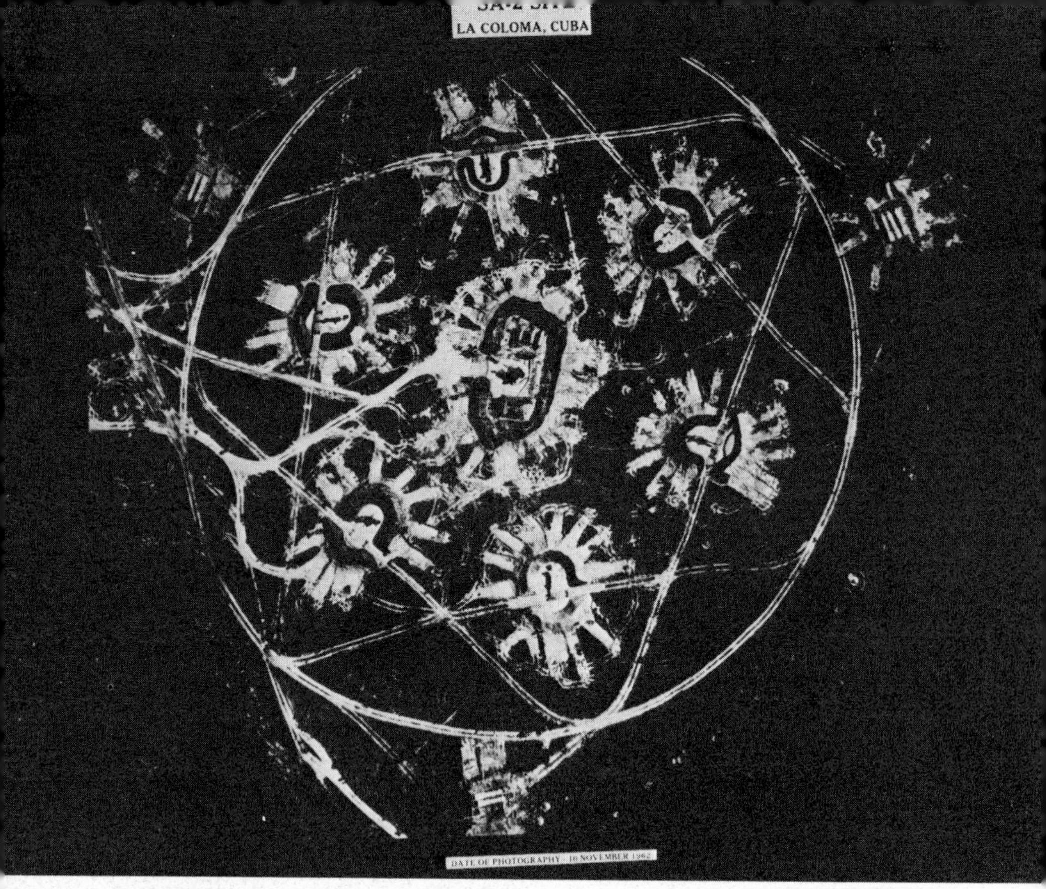

SA-2 SITE
LA COLOMA, CUBA

DATE OF PHOTOGRAPHY—10 NOVEMBER 1962

Typical of the photographs brought back from reconnaissance flights over Cuba, this USAF picture shows SA–2 ('Guideline') surface-to-air missile sites, with weapons emplaced. Purpose of such installations was to protect the launch areas where long-range bombardment missiles were being located. Date of photography was November 10th 1962.

Deck cargo of the freighter *Komsomol*, found and photographed by the USAF, included intermediate-range bombardment rockets bound for Cuba. Other ships carried Il–28 bombers.

Unfortunately, these two requirements are not compatible in conventional aircraft. Great altitude needs power, and power means weight, and the combination of power and weight is the enemy of range. Conventionally, also, extensive range needs vast quantities of fuel, and this again spells weight.

Faced with a seemingly impossible task, Kelly Johnson came up with answers that, according to the pundits, were quite impossible. His aircraft would, he said, fly at more than 70,000ft (21,300m). That was a pipe-dream for starters; the world altitude record for aeroplanes stood at only 56,046ft (17,083m), set up by the Italian Mario Pezzi in a specially-prepared Caproni 161 *bis*.

It would be powered, said Johnson, by a jet engine. That was perhaps the biggest laugh of all: even a non-expert could tell you that a turbojet was so fuel-thirsty that long range was the last thing it could provide.

Johnson must have listened with considerable amusement. He knew—and he alone—that, however far-fetched his ideas might sound, he could achieve success. This, of course, is the stuff of which great designers are made. High technical integrity and the knowledge of problems solved, breeds a kind of super-skill, a sixth sense, a sureness.

When he put his proposition to the USAF early in 1954 it was rejected. We don't know why, and can only conjecture that its leaders did not then appreciate the need for the information that such an aircraft would give them; that they were staggered at the sum of money needed to develop so unconventional an aeroplane; or that they were afraid of the unconventionality itself.

Only the growing need to learn what developments were taking place behind the Iron Curtain brought a change of opinion, fostered by the more far-sighted who appreciated that such knowledge was essential for the security of the Western world. In December 1954 the USAF gave approval and in the 'Skunk Works', at Burbank, Kelly Johnson's 'miracle' began to take shape.

Its shape was not very unusual, for it had the configuration of a fairly normal mid-wing monoplane. The unconventionalities came in its construction.

Prime requirement was light weight, so that a single turbojet engine could lift it to unprecedented heights. This meant that the airframe's component parts had to be made of the thinnest-gauge material that would preserve structural integrity. It left no margin for heavy landings or violent manoeuvres. It dictated also a special landing gear, of bicycle type, with single wheels fore and aft. To balance it on the ground it had 'pogos', a lightweight strut and wheel device, located in a socket under each wingtip. Neither was there a heavy ejection seat: in emergency the pilot had to 'bail out' over the side in classic manner.

The all-important question of range was resolved by building, in effect, a powered glider. By shutting down the turbojet engine, and gliding for long periods of flight, the U-2, as it became known, was able to traverse remarkable distances at heights beyond the reach of contemporary fighters or defensive missiles.

This, then, was the aircraft which represented one of the most important weapons ever built for clandestine operations when it began to enter service in 1956.

The availability of such an aircraft was useless, of course, without the means to record the activity taking place on the ground, thousands of feet below its invisible course in the upper air.

Primarily responsible for development of the sophisticated cameras carried by the U–2 was Dr Edwin Land. It was he who had made available to the general public a revolutionary camera, known originally as the Land camera, which could take and develop almost instantaneous positive prints of family snaps. To the general public it is better known as the Polaroid camera, a frequent recorder of holiday scenes.

He produced for the U–2 a special long-focus camera which, scanning continuously through seven apertures, was able to record a 125-mile (200km) strip of land beneath the aircraft's track. So remarkable was the ability of this camera to capture minute detail that in a reconnaissance photograph, released for publication in the early days of the U–2 programme, showing a golf course 55,000ft (16,800m) below the camera's eye, it was possible to pick out golf balls on a putting green.

But cameras alone do not provide the information needed in an electronic age. The U–2 carried also a full quota of 'black boxes', to provide information, among other things, on radio and radar equipment used by the country over which the aircraft was operating.

With the aircraft and its equipment available, a decision had to be made whether it was politic to use it for overflights of the Soviet Union. This was no easy matter to decide; one of the principal reasons which enabled the American President to give his approval was Soviet rejection of the Open Skies policy. As the major military power of the Western nations, it was felt that in the vital interest of maintaining world peace America had no option but to gather whatever information she could about the military potential of the Soviet Union. She would then, at any time, be able to meet force with at least equal force.

Special 'planes need special pilots, in more ways than one. Those for the U–2 required not only exceptional skills in their chosen field, but stamina, dedication to their dangerous task and, of prime importance because of the secret nature of the proposed operations, they had to be a first-class security risk. Some of them came from the USAF, others from civilian sources. Those from the Air Force had to resign their commissions and become civilians for the term of their contract. All came under the control of the Central Intelligence Agency (CIA).

Their first task was to learn to fly the U–2 and this, as one can imagine, was easier said than done. Take-off presented no real problem, for the bicycle landing gear was augmented by the wingtip 'pogos', which kept the wings level until flying speed had been attained. As the aircraft left the ground the 'pogos' fell away. They were responsible, however, for one fatal accident early in the training programme. As that particular aircraft left the ground one 'pogo' remained firmly in its socket. The pilot made a pass over the airfield at low level and tried, by waggling the wings, to shake it free. In doing so he lost control and the aircraft became a wreck.

Once airborne, the U–2 climbed like a thoroughbred. At extreme altitude it displayed a temperamental characteristic of a thoroughbred, for the margin of speed between maximum and stalling was frighteningly small. Its pilots needed a high degree of concentration to maintain a secure hold on their 'tightrope' in the sky.

Landing presented the pilot with completely new problems. Having consumed its load of fuel, the combination of light weight and large wing area meant that the U–2 was reluctant to leave its natural element and get back to Mother Earth. It virtually had to be stalled, at just the right height, if it was to be prevented from bouncing back into the air again. And once on the ground the problems were not yet over, for it had to be balanced critically on its two wheels until speed was low enough for it to topple over on to a wingtip skid and come to rest without expensive damage.

Because of the need to limit weight to a minimum, the U–2 had no pressurisation system to provide a safe environment for its pilot at extreme altitude. This meant that the pilot had to wear a tightly-fitting airtight semi-pressure suit, his head encased in a 'goldfish bowl' that was hermetically sealed to the suit. He breathed pure oxygen, under pressure—easy enough to inhale but difficult to exhale, involving him in learning to breathe in a new and unnatural way, for hours at a time.

Eventually, men and machines were ready for the exciting job that had required so much preparation. Late in 1956 they were transferred, officially as meteorological observation squadrons—one to Incirlik AFB, at Adana in Turkey, another to Wiesbaden in West Germany.

Operations began with electronic surveillance flights along the Russian borders, and one might imagine that these were little more than proving or operational training flights. This was not so. They were, as flights of this nature still are, highly valuable in providing a wealth of important intelligence.

Flying at great height, silent and invisible, they gained information that made it possible to pinpoint many Russian military installations. They were able also to learn much about test launchings of Soviet rockets. By taking atmospheric samples at high altitude soon after a nuclear test, it was possible for American scientists to gather a mass of data for calculations that showed the type of weapon, its destructive potential and the source of the explosion. Valuable, indeed, at a time when the West needed to know so much about Russian progress in the atomic arms race.

In due course the decision was made to begin overflights of Soviet territory. The border flights had provided a great deal of knowledge, but only photographic reconnaissance added to electronic surveillance would supply a complete and satisfactory picture of events taking place behind the Iron Curtain.

By this time, the U–2 unit in Turkey had been supplemented by that which had been operating in West Germany. This latter unit had already moved once, for security reasons, to Giebelstadt. But when pilots reported a suspicious-looking car parked too often near the end of the runway, and found that it belonged to an embassy of the 'other side', it was considered more discreet to operate from Adana. A third unit was also established at Atsugi, Japan, in 1957.

The pilots briefed for the early overflights were faced with a large number of unknown and worrying factors. It was not known, for example, whether Russian defences had the capability at that time of locating and attacking the spy-planes. There was no doubt of the fact that they had made considerable advances in radar and that they possessed large numbers of surface-to-air missiles. The effective altitude and guidance accuracy of these latter weapons were completely unknown factors.

With height as their only defence, it was necessary to provide the pilots with means of survival in the event that any of the U–2s were intercepted successfully. A seat-pack attached to the parachute harness housed the more conventional items, such as water, food, flares and first aid kit. Each pilot had also a hunting knife and a pistol, and was offered a cyanide capsule 'just in case'. To protect the more secret equipment carried in the aircraft there was an explosive device which could be operated by the pilot when bailing out of his aircraft. It had a delay mechanism that was supposed to allow him time to make his escape after setting to 'destruct'. Even the most naive pilot was aware that such mechanisms were not too reliable. Extreme height might make them temperamental.

Nevertheless, the overflights began well. They proved to be something of a 'milk run' so far as detection and interception were concerned. The real problem was the physical and emotional strain of being confined within a pressure suit for anything up to ten hours, seated in a cramped cockpit and forced to breathe in a manner contrary to nature.

The pilots could see little if anything of the territory below. They concentrated on maintaining with great accuracy a predetermined course, activating cameras and other special equipment at points or times for which they had been briefed with great care. They knew little of the results, of whether or not their flights were gaining the necessary intelligence.

As they learnt at a later date, they were. So much so that the chief of the CIA during that period was able to comment in retrospect that the capability of the U–2 ". . . could be equalled only by the acquisition of technical documents directly from Soviet offices and laboratories . . . (it) marked a new high, in more ways than one, in the scientific collection of intelligence."

For example, there had long been controversy in Western military circles as to whether manned bombers or long-range missiles were the best means of retaliation in the event of war. The argument always seemed to end up with the factor that since the Russians were busy building up their bomber force it was unnecessary to become involved in the astronomical costs of developing and building immense numbers of intercontinental ballistic missiles (ICBMs).

In July 1955, U–2s maintained a bird's-eye view of the Soviet Aviation Day fly-past over Moscow. Observers on the ground were staggered as squadron after squadron of heavy bombers flew past in review. Their numbers far exceeded anything that Western intelligence had estimated. Amazement turned to concern as they continued to thunder past; ears became deaf with the never-ending roar of jet engines.

Only the U–2s could tell the true story, of a limited number of bombers that turned, when out of sight, made a circle and tagged on to the end of the column. They were able to prove also that, while the Western nations were happy in the belief that the Soviet Union had been concentrating on bomber production, the 'other side' had, in reality, been busy developing and building long-range missiles.

The West had been too trusting for too long. The U–2 provided the truth, fortunately before it was too late. If there were those who doubted the information gained by the spy-planes, they learnt the error of their beliefs when in August 1957 the Russians announced that they had an ICBM in service: they were probably shattered when, on October 4th of the same year, the Soviet *Sputnik I* satellite was launched successfully into Earth orbit.

The U–2 flights continued and, with the passing of time, various modifications were incorporated. Because there had been problems in bailing-out from disabled aircraft an ejection seat was added; and as the need for additional electronic surveillance grew, so did the number of black boxes. This meant, inevitably, that the take-off weight of the aircraft was on the increase, and in 1959 a more powerful engine was installed to enable the aircraft to maintain the high altitudes that alone spelt safety.

One of these new versions force-landed near its base in Japan and was quickly surrounded by interested spectators, busily photographing this unusual aeroplane. When US military police arrived and dispersed the crowd at gunpoint questions were asked.

A prominent Japanese aviation journalist, Eiichiro Sekigawa,* posed some pertinent questions in an aviation magazine, querying the lack of identification letters or insignia and the need to use strong-arm tactics to turn back the civilians. Its purpose, he argued, must be clandestine.

The secret of the U–2s began to leak out in other ways. Most surprising, perhaps, was information that appeared in an aeromodellers' magazine, which reported that the U–2s were being used to fly beyond the Iron Curtain to take reconnaissance photographs of Russian military installations.

Knowledge of the fact that the Soviet Union must now be aware of the overflights, and their purpose, did little to ease the strain on the pilots

* Author of *A Pictorial History of Japanese Military Aviation* in preparation.

flying the missions. It soon became clear also that the Russians were tracking their course by radar, and some pilots reported that surface-to-air missiles had been sighted though, as yet, they had not reached a threatening altitude. The only defence was, so far as possible, to avoid known SAM installations. Time was running out for the U–2.

At 05.20 hours on May 1st 1960, the U–2 pilot whose name would soon be known internationally was climbing into the cockpit of his aircraft at Peshawar, Pakistan. Ahead was a route of some 3,800 miles (6,120km), across Afghanistan to Murmansk, around the northern coasts of Finland and Sweden, with Bodö in Norway as his landing point. It was to be the first complete overflight of the Soviet Union from South to North. It was not lack of range that had prevented an earlier attempt at such a flight; the problems involved in taking off from one base and landing at another, some thousands of miles away, had been considered too great unless the potential reward was worthwhile.

Despite the early hour it was already very hot by the time Powers had settled in the cockpit of his aircraft and had completed his pre-flight checks. Although he was due to take off at 06.00 hours, it was not until 06.20 hours that he received clearance. By this time the woollen underwear beneath his pressure suit was soaked in perspiration: his head, already sealed within the 'goldfish bowl', added rivulets of sweat that trickled uncomfortably down his neck.

At 06.26 hours he was away, soon feeling chilled as the U–2 gained height, and it was not long before he was across the border. Beyond some trouble with his autopilot the flight was proving routine: by the time he was approaching Sverdlovsk he had passed the half-way mark and it seemed he would complete his mission without incident. Then came the terrifying moment when the Russian SAM knocked his aircraft out of control.

Powers was a rare prize for the Communists, and he was questioned endlessly in Lubyanka Prison until the end of June. On Wednesday August 17th he was brought to trial in the Hall of Columns in Moscow. Everything possible had been done to ensure maximum publicity, for at last Premier Krushchev had exactly what he needed to discredit the United States, enabling him to claim that this overt act represented an aggressive provocation aimed at wrecking the Summit Conference.

Roman Rudenko, the prosecutor, had much to add in similar theme, claiming the Soviet Union as a society of Communists who were engaged in peaceful creative labour and a people who abhorred war. The US, on the other hand, was stubbornly opposing measures for universal disarmament. The fantasy continued until, on August 19th, Powers was sentenced to ten years' imprisonment.

Happily, he had only served about twenty months of this term when, on February 10th 1962, he was liberated in a dramatic exchange for the Soviet spy, Col Rudolf Abel, who had been held by the Americans.

Had the results of the U–2 flights, the embarrassment of the US over the Powers affair and the resulting increase in East–West tension been worthwhile? Of course they had. President Eisenhower summed it up neatly when he said "Aerial photography has been one of the many methods we have used to keep ourselves and the Free World abreast of major Soviet military developments. The usefulness of this work has been well established through four years of effort. The Soviets were well aware of it. The plain truth is this: when a nation needs intelligence activity, there is no time when vigilance can be relaxed."

Although the overflights of the Soviet Union had ended with Powers' capture, the value of the amazing U–2 aircraft had not reached a climax. In addition to ferreting out secrets of Soviet rocket launchings, and the development of Red China's nuclear capability, and scientific studies of high-altitude winds and weather phenomena, the U–2 continues in service for other tasks, its true performance still classified information.

We shall see, in the next chapter, how 'Kelly' Johnson's creation played its part in preventing a third World War: no mean achievement for a mere reconnaissance aircraft.

# 8 On the Brink of World War III

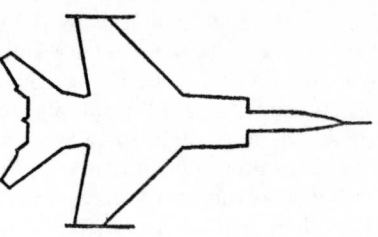

On an Autumn day in the year 1962, lying on a viewing table in America's secret National Photographic Interpretation Center was the evidence of a confrontation that had seemed inevitable since that moment, just over fourteen years earlier, when the Soviet Union had closed the surface routes to and from Berlin.

A casual inspection of the prints that covered the table would have revealed nothing to a layman. Only the practised eye of a highly skilled photographic interpreter (PI) could read the evidence that confirmed the presence of medium-range ballistic missile sites. The fact that these missiles had been installed on the Communist-controlled island of Cuba, and that they were trained against the industrial area of the north-east United States, caused an immediate national crisis.

The prints were rushed to the White House for inspection by President Kennedy who, after careful study, turned to an expert for confirmation of the evidence visible to his own eyes. Was there any doubt that the sites pinpointed by the photographs were those of ballistic missiles? None!

In his Inaugural Address in January 1961, President John F. Kennedy had said "In the long history of the world, only a few generations have been granted the role of defending freedom in its hour of maximum danger. I do not shrink from this responsibility. . . ."

The hour of maximum danger had come, in a world which possessed terrifying weapons that, if launched without just cause in a moment of panic, could end the slowly-won, long-drawn-out process of social development that we call civilisation.

A smattering of Cuba's more recent history is necessary for us to appreciate the whys and wherefores of the situation that had arisen.

In the period 1940–53 Cuba, largest and most populated island of the West Indies, had suffered the corrupt and inefficient dictatorship of Fulgencio Batista Saldivar, hated by Cubans of all classes. A revolt, initiated by Fidel Castro in July 1953, eventually overthrew the island's administration and Castro made a triumphal entry into Havana.

He lost little time in setting up a left-wing regime, having close ties with the Soviet Union and its teachings. As a result, Castro retained the loyalty of the peasant majority: a large proportion of the middle and upper class minority sought refuge in the US. With US support they planned a counter-revolution and in April 1961 had invaded Cuba from Florida. Their landing, in the Bay of Pigs, was short-lived and bloody.

Little wonder that US–Cuban relations had become increasingly embittered.

The U–2s, which had been busy gathering vital intelligence from bases in Turkey and Japan, were supplemented by those of the USAF's Strategic Air Command. From their airfield at Laughlin AFB, Del Rio, Texas, they were ready to keep a watchful eye on trouble spots anywhere in the world.

On August 29th 1962, a U–2 had been assigned to take a look at Cuba. This had become a routine task since the institution of the Castro regime. When the reconnaissance photographs had been developed, PIs soon identified the existence of surface-to-air missile sites. Further sorties, flown at lower level, confirmed that the SAMs were of Russian origin.

Since these missiles were defensive and not offensive weapons, there was little concern in US military circles. Only the director of the CIA had his finger firmly on the pulse of the situation when he commented that they presented little danger to the US ". . . except as a means of making possible the introduction of offensive missiles".

It was prudent after that to maintain an ever-watchful eye on the island, separated from the US coastline by the Florida Straits, spanning a distance of only some 150 miles (240km).

This was the situation when strange rumours began to circulate in the US. Traced back to source by good intelligence work, it transpired that Cuban refugees had spoken of strange objects shrouded in tarpaulins being unloaded at the docks from foreign ships. On being questioned they admitted that the objects were of considerable length and appeared to be of circular cross-section. Other rumours mentioned construction work at isolated sites; that people who had glimpsed these sites at too-close range had not been seen again; that ever-watchful eyes had noticed Russian cargo ships unloading strange freight by night. Cloak and dagger indeed.

The U–2 flights, which had been a mere twice-a-month routine, were stepped up immediately on the basis of these rumours and discovery of the surface-to-air missile sites. By early October extensive coverage of the island had been achieved. The photographs revealed more of the SAM sites, MiG fighters, whose presence had long been known, but nothing else. It seemed that the reports were plain old-fashioned rumours, and tension relaxed.

It happened, however, that one of the PIs, who had studied closely the photographs of the Soviet Union taken by U–2s operating from Adana, noticed that photographs of an area near the town of San Cristobal, on Cuba, had the surface-to-air missile sites deployed in a pattern similar to those in Russia. In this latter country such a set-up had pinpointed offensive missile sites.

He requested that the area be subjected to more detailed coverage and, after approval by higher authority, two U–2s were despatched to bring back photographic evidence of the area in question.

On October 14th these reconnaissance aircraft, operating at a height of about fifteen miles (24km), set about their task. There was the ever-present danger, in the forefront of all minds since the Powers' affair, that their mission might meet with opposition. In the event, they completed their task without alarms of any kind. On their return to base, the cameras were quickly unloaded and the magazines of film were rushed to Washington by a jet aircraft that had been standing by. It was the pictures from this sortie that eventually came to rest on President Kennedy's desk.

As one might imagine, the President's mind was full of questions to which he wanted, and had to have, as many positive answers. Questions like how many other sites were being built, how many missiles were involved, how soon could they be deployed against the United States?

The answers could only be supplied by reconnaissance aircraft. For the first time since East and West had both become nuclear-armed, the fate of the world depended upon the skill and courage of pilots flying unarmed aircraft (a type of vehicle designed originally for sport or a means of transportation) and the all-seeing eye of the camera (developed first to record things of beauty). Man has long rebelled against the corruption of peaceful inventions for military usage: the time had come for them to demonstrate their ability to preserve civilisation itself.

A massive reconnaissance operation was mounted. By day and night, specialised aircraft of the USAF and USN roamed the skies above Cuba and its sea approaches, recording and reporting anything and everything that might be significant.

By October 21st it was clear that the situation was critical, and President Kennedy realised it was essential to let the Soviet Union know that the United States was ready and able to meet force with force.

Before making such a grave pronouncement, it was necessary that the armed might of the US should be ready to unleash such devastating retaliation that only a maniac would dare light the fuse. Kennedy believed that the rulers of the Soviet Union would not take such a risk. He believed this to be so; he did not *know*. While many of us might envy a President his trappings of pomp, privilege or affluence, few would wish to carry the burden of such momentous decisions.

By way of preparation, the offensive and defensive forces of the United States were ordered to put into operation certain plans that had been drawn up for just such a contingency. The deadline for the completion of this preparatory stage was October 20th.

In the three days prior to this date, America was alive with the movements of men, ships and aircraft. Strategic Air Command's (SAC's) B–47 Stratojets and B–52 Stratofortresses combined with the Navy to track the movements of some 2,000 ships to-ing and fro-ing on the Atlantic Ocean. Not only were they carrying out an important task, either reporting visually or recording photographically the movement of shipping on this vast sea of communication: they were, at the same time, airborne and maintaining SAC's capability of nuclear strike. A target moving in three unknown dimensions is a very different proposition to the sitting duck on an airfield that has already been pinpointed by enemy intelligence.

Tactical Air Command had such an enormous task that it seemed as if three days would suffice only for the planning stage. Its job was to transport thousands of men, their equipment, supplies and weapons to bases in Florida. As if this were not enough, it had also to ensure that hospital and first aid facilities were available at convenient bases, and that almost one-and-a-half thousand blood transfusions were standing by.

Air Defense Command (ADC) made sure that it was ready to intercept or attack anything that moved on or from Cuba. Humorists, the essential bloodstream of any crisis, commented that ADC had moved so many aircraft into the south-eastern corner of the US that Florida had sunk two feet lower.

The USN was heavily committed, at sea and in the air: its task to police the now too-narrow Florida Straits and all sea approaches to the home country.

It was desperately necessary that America's allies should be made aware of the true facts of the situation. On October 21st President Kennedy despatched special couriers to France, West Germany and Britain. Armed with a selection of reconnaissance photographs, they were able to satisfy the leaders of these nations of the extent of Soviet influence in Cuba and of the gravity of the situation. None had doubts; all were aware that the United States must call the Russian bluff: if bluff it was.

On October 22nd Strategic Air Command made sure that it was in a position to mount a maximum nuclear retaliation. Its operational fleet of B–52s was split in two: half were airborne, the other half relieving them in the air when they were forced to land. At the same time, all of SAC's intercontinental ballistic missile sites were confirmed at a constant state of readiness. The whole of America's offensive and defensive force was ready—for anything.

On that day, Monday October 22nd 1962, President Kennedy gave the score to the Soviet Union in an historic broadcast, announcing that he was initiating a policy of examination of all shipping, of any nation, bound for Cuba. All vessels would be stopped and their cargo examined: if it included offensive weapons the ship would not be allowed to proceed.

He warned that he had ". . . directed the Armed Forces to prepare for any eventualities; and I trust that, in the interest of both the Cuban people and the Soviet technicians at the sites, the hazards to all of continuing this threat will be recognised. . . ."

To make sure that the Soviet leaders would be completely certain of his intentions, he concluded: "It shall be the policy of this nation to regard any nuclear missile launched from Cuba against any nation in the Western Hemisphere as an attack by the Soviet Union on the United States, requiring a full retaliatory response upon the Soviet Union. . . ."

The cards were on the table.

Throughout the world tension mounted. Peace was balanced on a knife-edge. Was the deterrent policy capable of keeping the two great military powers from each other's throats?

This was, perhaps for the first time, a moment when weapons could achieve nothing at all. Nothing, that is, but annihilation. Only America's fleet of reconnaissance aircraft was in a position to monitor the situation: continuously. Only the camera's eye could determine whether Soviet pressure was being increased to a point where, whatever the consequences, the US President would be forced to take irrevocable action.

High-altitude reconnaissance by the U-2s was stepped up yet again, and to provide more detailed coverage low-level sorties were flown by RF-101 Voodoos of the USAF and RF-8A Crusaders of the USN. These latter aircraft, of the Navy's VFP-62 Squadron, had the unenviable task of keeping a close watch on the missile sites in an attempt to discover whether they were at stand-by or if, at any time, there were signs that the missiles were being put in an advanced state of readiness.

The 1,000mph (1,610km/h)-plus Crusader, built by Ling-Temco-Vought, had previously achieved an amazing reconnaissance record. One, piloted by Marine John Glenn (who later became known internationally as the first American astronaut to be placed in Earth orbit) had been the first aircraft to span the American continent faster than the speed of sound, simultaneously making a reconnaissance map of an area across the whole nation.

Before the Crusaders could take off on a mission of this nature special electronic crews had to prepare the automatic cameras to operate at the right speed, angle and timing, and ensure that the film magazines were loaded with the right film for the job in hand.

Thundering low over the Cuban missile sites, the pilots had no easy task. Despite the flashing speed, they had to maintain accurate courses at heights that were often below treetop level; at the same time, they had to be constantly on the alert for offensive action from the enemy. Flying such machines demands precise and positive action; there is no time to dither when your wingtips are only feet from the ground.

Throughout their sweep over the island the cameras in the Crusaders were busy clicking away at a speed of several shots a second, made at precise intervals so that the resulting prints would overlap slightly and reveal details at differing angles. This enabled a PI to examine the prints through a stereo viewer—though many experienced PIs can view stereo-scopically without special equipment by separating (rather than crossing) their eyes—enabling them to see objects in relief instead of the flat shape from a single photograph.

The technique is for the PI to scan a roll of film until he finds the particular area that he wants to study in detail. This is repeated with other rolls of film until he is able to select sufficient photographs to build up a mosaic of the area and its immediate terrain. Only then can he begin his microscopic study, putting together odds and ends of clues to permit a reasoned interpretation of the activity in that area. A mound of earth might suggest excavations for missile or ammunition storage: deep tracks in a dirt road can provide an accurate indication of the weight of a vehicle's load; if another shot showed a missile being unloaded it would be possible to estimate its range. Such is the scope of the photographic interpreter.

In the Cuban crisis so much depended on these men. As soon as the Crusaders landed back at base their film magazines were rushed to the squadron processing team who, using special mobile equipment, could develop 600ft (183m) of roll film an hour and produce up to 30,000 prints a day.

With such a flood of prints there was soon an enormous backlog of work for the PIs. Throughout the Cuban crisis a small army of them kept hard at it by day and night. But despite the vast number of prints that were processed and examined, and despite the most careful and hopeful interpretation of the story they had to tell, the situation remained unchanged.

Throughout the world ordinary men and women, without specialised knowledge or an appreciation of the finer points of diplomacy, were agreed that a condition of threatening stalemate existed. Time and time again they listened to news broadcasts, always hoping to hear of some indication that the Communists were backing down. But not a single statement came from the Russians. In this case no news was bad news: there were few who did not fear that the Soviet Union was preparing to meet the American challenge—and if it did would the Americans fight?

The question marks hung in the air for almost a week—one which passed on leaden wings. On Saturday October 27th there had still been no word from the Russians, and during that morning came an event which shocked the White House. One of the reconnaissance U–2s, making a routine check on Cuban missile sites—to determine any change in operational status— was destroyed by a ground-to-air missile.

The U–2 had been under constant surveillance from the moment of its take-off from McCoy AFB in Florida. The controllers, tracking the course of the U–2 by radar, were aware of the situation immediately it happened, and the grave news was flashed to the White House.

Was this the opening salvo of the third World War? Had the U–2 flown too close to missile sites that were readying their weapons for a devastating attack? Were the missiles trained—or on their way? With superb calm the Americans sat and waited.

This was the classic incident that had been feared since the birth of the deterrent concept. If, in retaliation for this single, perhaps thoughtless, action the US had initiated a reflex offensive of any size, the catastrophe of a nuclear war might have swept the globe.

Instead, Kennedy chose to increase the state of the nation's strike potential. That evening, at US bomber bases around the world, aircraft were loaded with nuclear weapons and placed at instant readiness. It needed only one more provocative move by some trigger-happy individual to loose the dogs of war.

Instead, on the following morning, came the relief for which the world had prayed. Over the Soviet radio Premier Krushchev announced that orders had gone out to dismantle the missile sites. The weapons were to be placed on board ships and returned to Russia. He could not resist a statement to the effect that weapons had been sent to Cuba only as a defensive measure.

Unfortunately, the American President and his advisers could not—and did not—share the depth of relief that swept around the world. Their position, as leaders of the major Western power, meant they could not relax their vigilance until the Russian statement of intent became fact. After all, there was no proof that the Russians would keep their word. It might merely be a bluff to gain time for an unexpected counter-move.

Once again, only reconnaissance aircraft could discover the true facts, and it was not long before they were criss-crossing the Cuban skies in search of convincing proof that the Russians were keeping their word.

A pair of RF–101 Voodoos of the USAF's 29th Tactical Reconnaissance Squadron was assigned to vet the important installations near San Cristobal. Great care was taken in briefing the pilots for this mission: if all was well it would prove a milk-run, if not they would probably be on the receiving end of a hail of anti-aircraft fire.

The two aircraft approached the island at low-level, hoping to avoid radar detection. Immediately they met the land they began hedge-hopping to their target, the thunder of their jet engines scattering people and animals in all directions. With cameras blinking their eyes at the scene below, they rocketed over the target, only to be met by defensive fire from the anti-aircraft batteries. Fortunately, no hits were registered and within seconds they were out of sight, heading back for their home base.

What did this action mean? The information was radioed to base and the tension began to mount again. As the Voodoos touched down on the home runway, cars raced to meet them to collect and rush their film magazines for processing.

At last the negatives were developed, and the prints ready for examination. They revealed, without doubt, that the Russians had kept their word. The missile sites were being dismantled.

The deterrent policy had worked. Soon the US forces were being despatched to their normal bases and the world knew that, by a hairsbreadth, the third World War had been averted.

It remained only for aerial reconnaissance to confirm that the rundown of Russian arms on Cuba was continued and that the weapons were loaded for transhipment back to Russia.

Since that time, constant watch has been maintained on the island to ensure that no more secret build-ups of offensive weapons will ever take place. Anything at all suspicious has been checked and double-checked by high- and low-level reconnaissance. In this way, America makes sure that no new threat is mounted.

In retrospect, the Cuban crisis emphasised the peace-keeping power of aerial surveillance. It gave the world an impressive demonstration of the potential of the Open Skies policy that had been proposed by President Eisenhower. No longer was it possible to argue that reconnaissance aircraft could find useful employment only in times of war. The aviation pioneers would have cheered to a man could they have known that the vehicle they gave to the world, as a new and exciting means of communication, had been able to preserve mankind from a horrifying end.

# 9 Vietnam, and the Quiet Ones

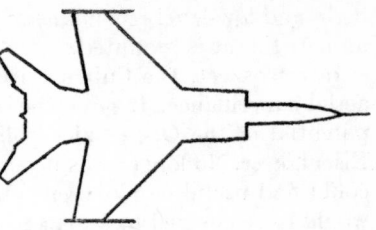

Solitary and serene, the little Bird Dog aircraft was cruising effortlessly above a seemingly green and prosperous land. Sunlight and a cloudless blue sky added to the illusion of peace. The Bird Dog, built by Cessna Aircraft in America, could be mistaken easily for just one more of the vast number of popular lightplanes produced by this manufacturer.

A closer look would have revealed that its purpose was not simply to provide a joy-ride for its pilot. Warlike camouflage and military insignia indicated far more serious business. Indeed, its pilot was known as a Forward Air Controller (FAC), and his job was to police a particular area of the countryside below. Every feature of the terrain had to be as familiar as the back of his own hand so that, by day or night, he could see—or sense—any change, however slight, in the normal aspect of the scene.

Right now he was making a daily routine flight, carefully scanning the countryside below. A glint of metal in a forest clearing attracted his attention: he pulled the Bird Dog into a gentle bank to port and, maintaining height, circled and watched. It seemed that he was mistaken, but there was no harm in trying the effect of a smoke grenade.

He tightened the bank, then levelled off to pass directly over the clearing: grenade in hand, he gripped the ring of the safety pin in his teeth, drew the pin, and lobbed the grenade out of the port window. Soon, crimson smoke was billowing over the lush green of the trees. This technique, known colloquially as 'recon by smoke', was often sufficient to get the enemy on the run, fearing that the pillar of smoke was a marker for more serious attack. This time it evoked no response.

Just to make sure, the FAC made a 180° turn and put the little machine into a shallow dive so that he could take a final low-level look at the clearing. He peered intently through the windshield for any sign of tell-tale movements.

Sudden flashes from the muzzle of a machine-gun confirmed his suspicions as reaction, trained to hair-trigger response, threw the Bird Dog into a steep climbing turn. Tracer followed his movements, far too close for comfort, but practised evasive action had him quickly out of range.

He resumed his gentle bank, circling the area as he called base for a

(Top) This USAF 2nd Air Division aerial reconnaissance photo shows a Vietnamese fortified outpost, 30 miles from Saigon, burning after a night attack by Vietcong guerrilla forces. Without constant observation, flare drops and tactical air support, hamlets and outposts were terribly vulnerable to such assault.

(Above) Shown here over Korea in 1952, the little Cessna O–1 Bird Dog later pioneered hazardous but rewarding forward air control operations in Vietnam.

Strange shapes are born of the modern demands for spy-planes, ECM aircraft, machines that can take-off almost anywhere, slow-fly during armed reconnaissance or perform one of a dozen other new or secret military tasks. The original Canberra design is barely discernible in the RB–57F 'weather reconnaissance' aircraft evolved from it.

The twin-turboprop North American OV–10A Bronco was conceived as an answer to the need for a specialised light armed reconnaissance, helicopter escort and forward air control combat aircraft for use in Vietnam. /Peter M. Bowers

Lockheed's YO–3A combines elements of the airframe of a Schweizer SGS 2–32 sailplane with a 210hp Continental engine, infra-red sensors and other, secret equipment. Object was to produce a machine which could fly quietly over a battle area at night without being spotted from the ground. /*Roy Lock*

Predecessor of the YO–3A was the Lockheed Q-Star, the ultimate development of which was this US Navy X–26B. The first machines of the series flew over Vietcong units in Vietnam at a height of only 100ft without being detected. /*Howard Levy*

(Above) Another way-out American descendant of the Canberra is the Westinghouse-modified B–57G, with nose-mounted radar, laser range-finder, TV camera and infra-red equipment for locating ground targets at night.

(Right) SMASH (South-east Asia Multi-sensor Armament System for HueyCobra) includes a nose-mounted infra-red sighting system and wing-mounted moving target indicator radar for all-weather day/night location of ground targets for attack.

(Above) This reconnaissance photograph revealed five MiG fighters in revetments near Kep airfield, 38 miles from Hanoi. Three of them were destroyed in a subsequent strike, which also rendered the runway unserviceable. /USAF

(Left) Ground personnel have still to close the camera-bay doors of this RF–101 Voodoo as its pilot clambers aboard to begin his pre-flight cockpit check.

(Far left) F–105D Thunderchief fighter-bombers added a variety of novel stores to their regular operational loads in Vietnam. The underbelly pod on this one housed ECM devices to assist penetration to the target. /J. Geer

(Top) No two photographs of members of the Boeing C–135 'family' based in Japan seem to show similar patterns of bulges and antennae. Missions performed by aircraft like this RC–135M are shrouded in secrecy. /T. Matsuzaki

(Above) Tupolev Tu–95 ('Bear-D') maritime reconnaissance bomber of the Soviet Naval Air Force making a close inspection of the US attack carrier *John F. Kennedy*. /US Navy

(Top) US Navy Phantoms 'escort' a Soviet Tu–16 ('Badger') as it passes over their carrier, the USS *Kitty Hawk*, in the North Pacific. /US Navy

(Above) Reheat on, two RAF Lightnings race into the air from Leuchars to intercept a Russian ECM 'spy-plane' over the North Sea.

(Top) The underbelly reconnaissance pack carried by this RAF Phantom of No 54 Squadron houses cameras and side-looking radar.

(Above) Some of the different cameras which can be packed inside the nose of Sweden's Saab S 35E Draken supersonic reconnaissance aircraft.

(Top right) The long canister slung under the fuselage of the US Army's Grumman OV–1D Mohawk contains side-looking airborne radar (SLAR).

(Centre right) Drawn curtains at the cabin windows of this US Army Beechcraft RU–21D ensure darkness for the crew members who must interpret what its grotesque aerials pick up.

(Right) Five pods, under wings and fuselage, and an assortment of other excrescences house the ECM equipment carried by the Grumman EA–6B Intruder. Such aircraft are used to lead an attack force, jamming enemy electronic defence systems as they go.

(Above) The RAF's Hawker
Siddeley Harrier has brought
completely new standards
of efficiency to combat area
reconnaissance and attack.
Combining vertical take-off
capability with transonic
speed, it can carry cameras,
heavy-calibre guns, or
whatever the current
situation demands, in its
interchangeable equipment
packs.

(Right) The saucer radome
rotating slowly above the
fuselage of this Grumman
E–2A Hawkeye identifies it
as an airborne warning and
control system (AWACS)
aircraft. Early warning of an
air or surface attack can be
given much earlier by radar
searching from a height of
more than 20,000ft. The
AWACS aircraft also has
the capability to direct
fighter aircraft towards an
incoming target.

(Far right) Addition of a
second pilot's cockpit on
the SR–71B/C enables
aircrew to be trained for
sorties that might
encompass a whole
continent in one short flight.

In addition to underwing rocket packs and fuel tanks, and two gun-packs under its fuselage, the Harrier can carry a five-camera centreline reconnaissance pod. An F.95 camera is installed permanently in its nose.

Fastest aeroplane in service with any air force is the USAF's Lockheed SR–71A, which can cruise at Mach 3·2 at immense heights. It lacks the armament of Russia's MiG–23, which is primarily a fighter.

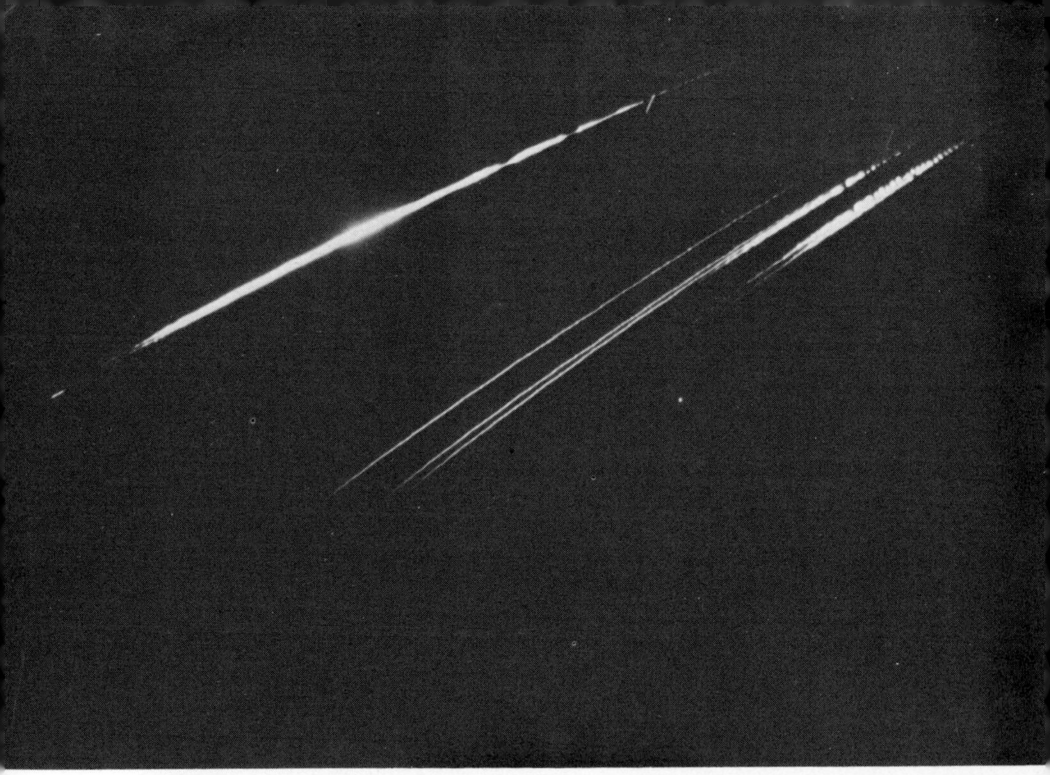

(Top) Photographic evidence that Russia is testing multiple re-entry vehicles on its SS–9 ICBM. Bright streaks at the top show booster parts burning up in the atmosphere. The three bottom streaks are from re-entry vehicles which would house the H-bomb warheads of an operational missile. /USAF

(Above) Equipment carried behind portholes in the cabin of aircraft like these much-modified C–135s enables the USAF to track and photograph incoming re-entry vehicles, 'friendly' or 'enemy'.

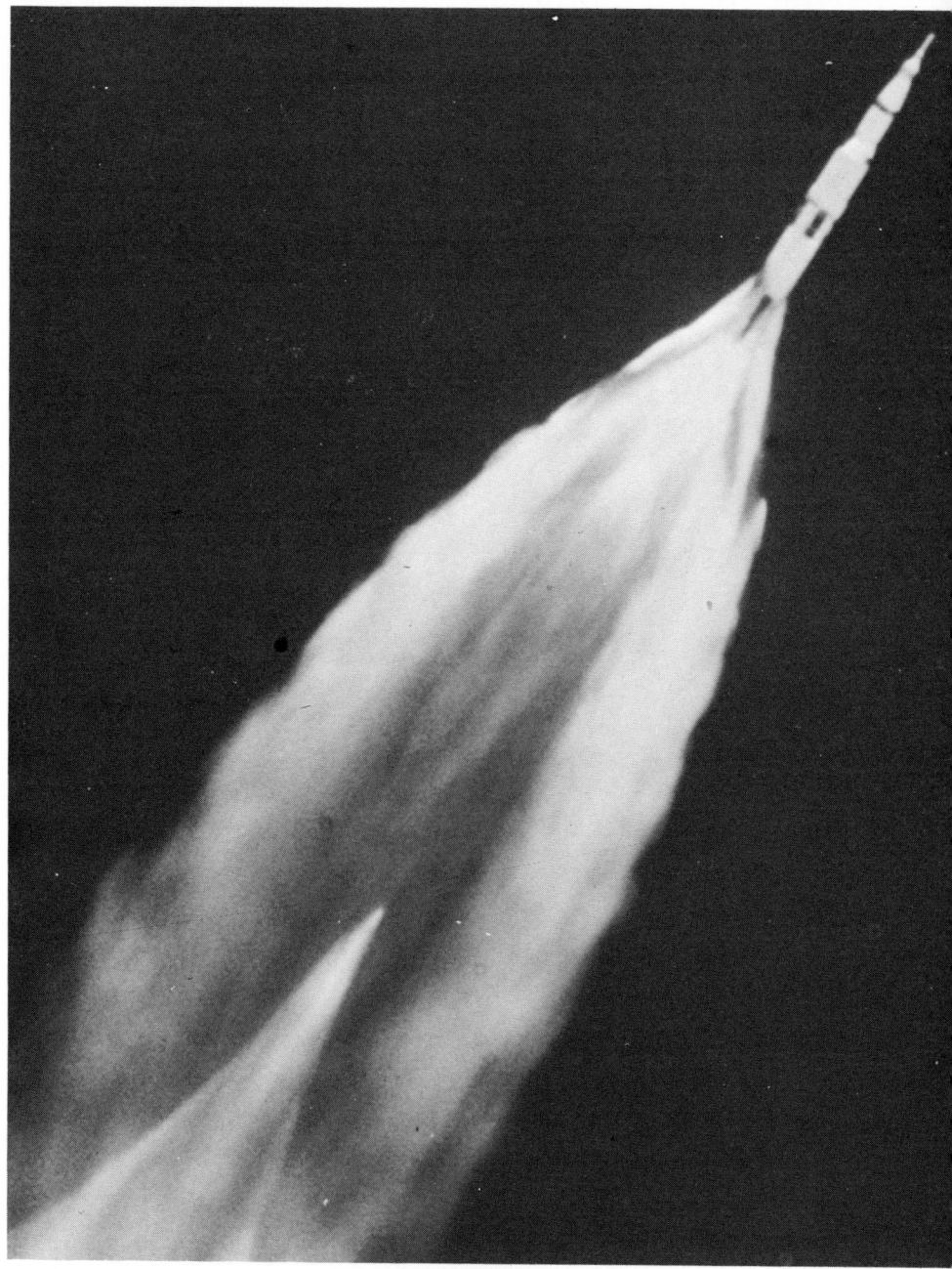

En route for the Moon, an Apollo spacecraft is photographed many miles above the Earth by an Airborne Lightweight Optical Tracking System (ALOTS) package on a USAF EC–135N aircraft. Similar techniques can produce invaluable information on rocket tests over a radius of hundreds of miles. /NASA

The photographs on this page and opposite show the AN/USD–501 reconnaissance drone produced by Canadair for the armed forces of Canada, the UK and West Germany. The drone is launched from a short ramp mounted on a truck, with the aid of a solid-propellant rocket booster which jettisons after burn-out.

During a demonstration flight, the drone's position is indicated on a large map as it follows a three-leg course beginning and ending at Camp Shilo, Manitoba.

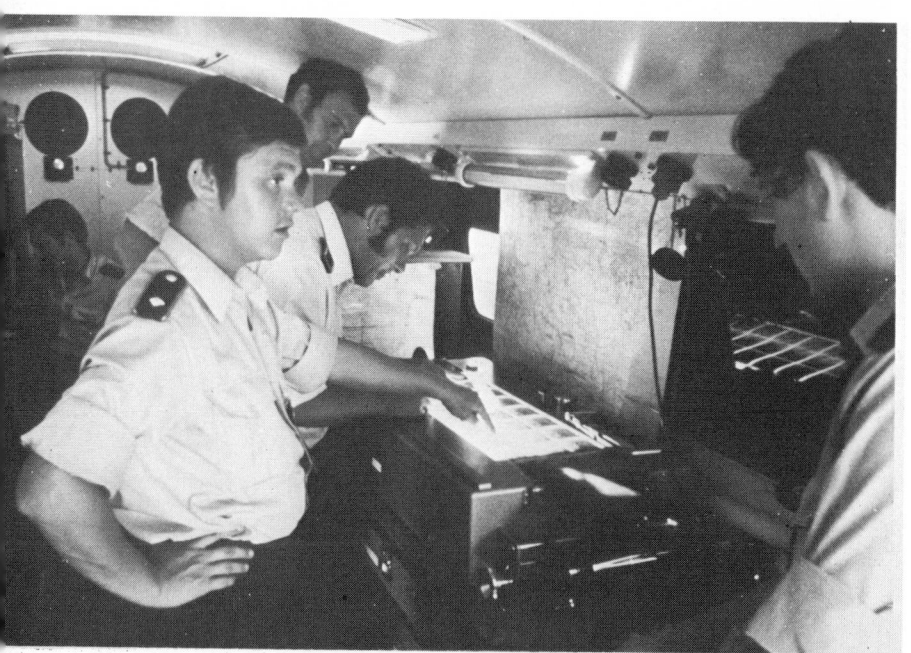

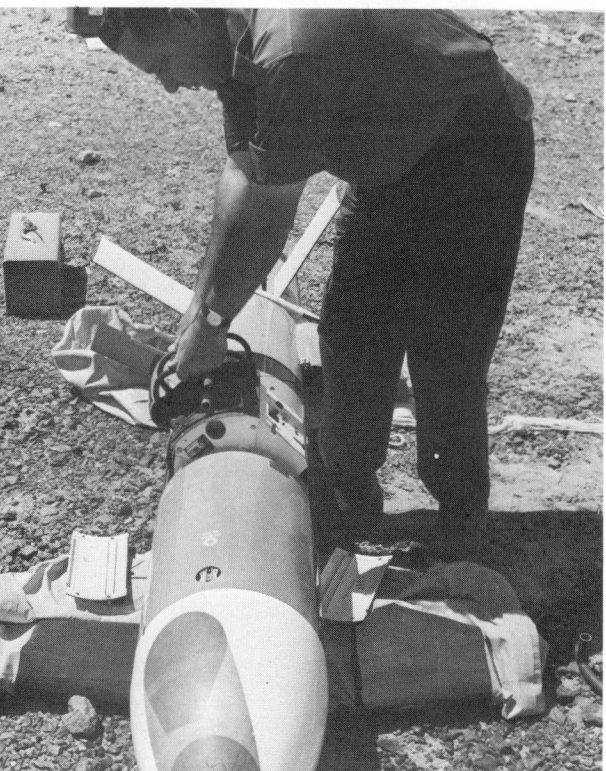

Discussing details shown on the photographs brought back from a typical sortie by an AN/USD–501.

Removing the sensor pack from an AN/USD–501 after recovery. Films are rushed to a mobile facility equipped with newly-developed rapid processing systems.

The German Dornier
Kiebitz (Peewit) mobile
reconnaissance/early
warning drone system. The
tethered 'flying platform'
positions itself up to 1,000ft
above its tracked ground
station.

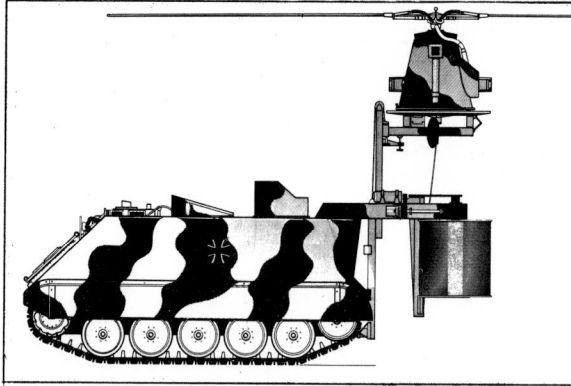

(Right) For transport the
Kiebitz packs into a
container at the rear of the
ground station, with its
rotor blades folded.

(Below) An early develop-
ment version of the Kiebitz
taking off from a truck
transporter/power station.

strike by F–100 Super Sabres. Within minutes, he was talking them into a position overhead.

"Can you see me now?", he asked. A disembodied voice in his earphones assured him of the fact by the single word "Roger". "Right. I'm going in in ten seconds." "Roger."

At the precise moment indicated by the second hand on his watch, he pulled up the Bird Dog's nose, flipped a wing over so that he was in a steep dive, and, as he lined the aircraft up, thumbed the firing button on his control column. With a whoosh of sound, clearly audible above the cockpit noise, a phosphorous rocket raced ahead, impacting a little to the left of the clearing.

"Target three o'clock, about 50 feet (15m) from smoke burst." Another "Roger" was the only reply. As he watched, two Sabres came knifing through the sky, levelling momentarily as silver canisters of napalm went hurtling down to straddle the clearing. The forest erupted in a great rolling cloud of flame and smoke. The Sabres came thundering back on a reciprocal course, nosing down into a dive as their 20mm cannon sprayed a vicious hail of death that went snapping and snarling through the tree-tops. There was no answering fire. Their job was done: with a dipping of wings in farewell, the Sabres headed for home in a low-level flurry of speed.

No such luck for the FAC. Like the local 'Bobby' on his beat he had a patrol to complete before he too, at a rather wistful hundred-odd miles per hour, could head for base and forget, until his next patrol, the vicious fight that never ended in the peaceful-looking countryside: the war in Vietnam.

To understand the origin of this continuing conflict we must go back to pre-World War II days, when France held colonial possessions known as Indo-China. These comprised Cambodia, Laos and the three provinces of Annam, Cochin-China and Tonking.

During the War these areas were occupied by the Japanese, and the strong nationalist movement that developed in this period was headed by the Communist-led Viet Minh.

France discovered after 1945 that if she wanted her colonies restored she would have to fight for them, so began to lose interest, as it was clear that the energetic Communists were more than a match for her war-weary troops. The ignominious surrender of some 16,000 men and their equipment at Diên Biên Phu on May 7th 1954 was the final straw.

A 14-nation conference, held at Geneva two months later, brought fighting to an end, and re-arranged the three former French provinces as two states—North and South Vietnam—their common frontier being the 17th parallel. North of the line belonged to the Viet Minh; the south was to remain under French control. It was hoped, in the naive manner of conferences generally, that this would be sufficient to maintain peace, and that a subsequent election would unite the country.

The withdrawal of French military forces from the south in 1955 was the signal for a policy of infiltration from the north. It was clear to the Western powers that control of Vietnam would soon be in Communist hands. Only America was able and willing to oppose such a move. A policy that began with the provision of advice and equipment grew, over a ten-year period, to a bitter war that seems no nearer to a solution as these words are being penned in 1972.

The Cuban crisis, and the Korean War that preceded it, had demonstrated the military value of aerial reconnaissance. War in Vietnam is being fought over terrain that favours the guerrilla tactics of the Vietcong. They travel lightly loaded, under cover of the jungle, and are adept at exploiting the element of surprise. It is no exaggeration to say that practically every movement made by the Arvin (Army of Vietnam) troops demands aerial reconnaissance, and this has given new impetus to the expansion of ideas and equipment.

The FAC whose story opened this chapter is but a modern counterpart of the observer who, as we have seen earlier, spotted for and ranged artillery during the formative years of military aviation.

Fundamentally his task is still one of pure reconnaissance; the weapons he carries are not intended for offensive action, but are needed to mark clearly and unmistakably the target which can be obliterated 'by arrangement'. Nevertheless, there is always the individual for whom words like 'intended', 'impossible' and 'danger' have little real meaning. Such a person was Capt H. J. Pawlak of the 19th Tactical Air Support Squadron based at Biên Hoa.

On patrol in his Bird Dog which, incidentally, has the military designation O–1, this FAC spotted enemy movements near an outpost 'fort'. Taking a closer look, he was met with a hail of fire and quickly put distance between himself and the Vietcong while he evaluated the score. By radio he advised his base, calling for support, but it was clear to him that immediate action was necessary if the fort was not to be overrun.

His weapons consisted of four phosphorous marker rockets and a rifle, so he decided to use these to gain as much time as possible. As the Vietcong grouped for attack he went in low and put a rocket in their midst. As they scattered he let them have a few rounds of small-arms fire for good measure, and by repeated use of this technique kept them in a jittery state for nearly half-an-hour, by which time a wing of Skyraiders appeared on the scene and took over the job.

The FAC's true reconnaissance role is of great importance in this uneasy war. By day and night he covers an assigned area that, more often than not when viewed from the air, has an appearance of pastoral peace and contentment. Only the tell-tale signs of the unusual, like trampled pathways, new earthworks, hastily-smothered fires and more-than-average numbers of sampans on little-used waterways have a story for him, and him alone.

By night, the evidence of Vietcong movements is less easy to read.

Sometimes the enemy discloses his position by an unconcealed light in a sector of the FAC's 'beat' that he knows is uninhabited. More often the well-developed sixth-sense of the FAC tells him when to drop a flare to illuminate the scene below. If this reveals a brief glimpse of the enemy he is able to call for extended illumination from artillery batteries, if conveniently located, or can bring to the scene aircraft equipped with pyrotechnics to turn night into day.

Little wonder that FACs are hated by the Vietcong, and that those who fall into the enemy's hands never fight again.

It was realised long ago that the solo FAC in his little machine had a pretty heavy workload. A two-seat machine in which the observer could concentrate on his task, without having to fly the aircraft as well, would be especially valuable at night. This led to the introduction of another Cessna aircraft, the O–2, a military variant of the Model 337 Super Skymaster. With two engines in a unique 'push-pull' arrangement, it is faster and can carry a more offensive load of weapons. It has capacity, too, for 'eyes' of a different kind that can help its Forward Air Navigator (FAN) to 'see' in the dark.

Details of these electronic 'eyes' are still classified, but it is known that the O–2s have a device nicknamed the 'starlight scope' which, by intensifying weak light sources, allows the FAN to see what would otherwise be invisible.

The helicopter, which 'came of age' in the Korean War, has also developed a new maturity in Vietnam. Its important contributions as a combat weapon, transport, field ambulance and rescue device for both men and machines are not within the scope of this book. It is obvious, however, that its ability to fly at slow speed or hover over a particular point makes it an ideal reconnaissance platform. Helicopters have also developed a potent 'sting': they are able to carry rocket pods and miniguns that make them deadly to encounter when in an aggressive mood.

This combination has made them valuable allies of Arvin infantry moving through the treacherous countryside, where ground vision is often limited to yards. In a terrain where the enemy is operating in small, well-concealed groups, it is good to know that the 'choppers', clattering along beside you, are constantly on the look-out. They are able, at the least sign of movement, to release a hail of fire and call for help from men or machines. The former, carried by helicopters, can be put down where no conventional aircraft could land: the latter can provide an air strike of terrifying power.

The helicopters, too, have become better equipped to seek out the will-o-the-wisp enemy, one who without a weapon in his hand is difficult to differentiate from a fellow-countryman in opposition to the Vietcong. Again, much of their equipment is classified, but one strange reconnaissance device gives an inkling of the ingenuity of scientists who, in one way and another, make it possible to 'see' much of what the enemy would prefer to keep hidden.

The primary factor of any army is its manpower. However good its weapons they must, usually, be operated or carried by men. This particular device, nicknamed the 'people sniffer', looks for men. Carried often in Bell Hueys (a nickname derived from the original HU–1 designation of these helicopters) it is able to detect the presence of humans by sensing certain chemicals exuded by perspiration.

Used by night, when the enemy was pretty certain that he only had to lay low to escape detection, the Hueys would slop-slop over the countryside. A high reading on the special meter of the people sniffer told the crew that the enemy was close at hand, and they would then drop large quantities of tear gas to flush out the hidden troops. Once located, troop-carrying helicopters could be called in to encircle the enemy until daylight, when artillery or air strike could finish the job.

Choppers, of course, have their limitations. No matter how good their flight characteristics for a low-level reconnaissance role, their most ardent admirers must admit they are more than a little noisy. The combination of engine and rotor-blade noise advertises their approach from quite a long way off.

The kind of war being fought in Vietnam needs a lot of low-level reconnaissance; especially to ferret out small bands of guerrilla forces that, like snakes, move quickly and quietly through the densely wooded terrain. They are helped by their similarity to the defending South Vietnamese and, operating in their natural habitat, can infiltrate across the borders and behind their enemy's lines with comparative ease.

It was soon apparent that it was necessary to keep a far closer watch on the Vietcong during the hours of darkness, their favourite time to slip past forward patrols, which they would then stalk and ambush at a suitable moment. Unfortunately, the impossible was needed to cope with such a situation: a new kind of aircraft that could cruise just above the tree-tops— silently!

In 1966 Lockheed, in America, began to study the possibility of developing a specialised aircraft for such a task. The idea was to take the airframe of a sailplane and add an engine that was extremely well silenced. To reduce the noise of the propeller to a minimum it was decided to use a large-diameter multi-blade design that would be able to produce adequate traction at low rotational speed.

Two prototypes were built for evaluation under operational conditions and shipped to Vietnam. The technique was to approach the reconnaissance area under power—very quietly too—and then switch off the engine and glide silently and secretly at tree-top level. It worked: so well that these strange little machines were able to fly as low as 100ft (30m) above the enemy without being detected.

It was not long before Lockheed were busy developing a more sophisticated machine for use in Vietnam. Designated Q–26, this is equipped with special electronic sensors to detect enemy forces under the most adverse conditions. Most of the 'black-box' equipment carried by these 'planes is classified, but it is known that they have infra-red sensors that are critically sensitive to heat emission.

It is surprising just how much can be 'seen' by the infra-red technique, for the sensors can pinpoint anything that gives a measurable amount of heat. Roads, of course, soak up the sun's heat during the day and radiate more heat than the surrounding countryside at night. Trucks and tanks give off heat as they move, and camp fires, troop concentrations and, on occasion, individuals have been detected by this means. A jet aircraft on take-off leaves a distinctive heat pattern that can be recorded long after it has left the ground.

Thus, the Quiet Ones are a valuable addition to the reconnaissance forces, and it is not surprising that other manufacturers are turning their attention to production of even more sophisticated versions of these aircraft.

Reconnaissance in Vietnam has not been the unique prerogative of the US Army and Air Force. The Navy has also been involved, and because the eastern boundary of both North and South Vietnam is bordered by the sea it is possible for carrier-borne reconnaissance aircraft to play an important role.

The fact that the aircraft are based on carriers has eased their task a little and, at the same time, has helped to make their contribution more valuable. This is because their bases are mobile, and Naval aircraft have been able to take on extremely difficult targets in North Vietnam that would have been classed as suicide missions if mounted from Saigon or Biên Hoa.

One of the most valuable aircraft used by the Navy in Vietnam is the North American Rockwell RA–5C Vigilante, which comprises the airborne unit of an Integrated Operational Intelligence System (IOIS). This aircraft carries reconnaissance sensors; passive ECM; vertical, oblique and horizon-to-horizon scanning cameras; and side-looking radar. The two-man crew, pilot and navigator, can each concentrate on his own task: the former is aided by an advanced automatic flight control system, the latter by a radar-equipped inertial navigation system that pinpoints his position over featureless landscape.

Flying off carriers operating in the Gulf of Tonkin, the Vigilantes roar low over the sea and, guided by their superb navigation system, can make accurate low-level penetrations of the enemy coastline.

There is much for them to do and much for them to photograph. Surface-to-air missile (SAM) sites in particular need to be located accurately so that they can be avoided—or eliminated—by offensive aircraft seeking major targets in North Vietnam. This task has particular problems for which the Vigilante is well suited. It is fast, and when enemy gunners are alerted it can 'get to hell out of it' quicker than most. More importantly, because it carries an inertial guidance system, every photograph it takes is over-printed with the latitude and longitude at the moment of exposure. Subsequent location of important 'finds' is ridiculously easy.

When one of the Navy's RA–5Cs lands back on its carrier, the mass of information gathered by camera, radar and electronic sensors is processed as quickly as possible and fed into the IOIS, which is not only being updated constantly by each new reconnaissance sortie, but is providing a 'bank' of reconnaissance intelligence that, due to the sophistication of the system, is readily retrievable for operational requirements and planning.

The Vietcong have been quick to appreciate the extent to which the Americans have relied upon intelligence gained by their airborne 'eyes'. They have not only made every effort to keep their movements well concealed, but have learned to identify reconnaissance aircraft and regard them as prime targets.

Some of their concealment has been fiendishly clever. For example, the area around Hanoi is veined with fast-flowing rivers that can be crossed only by bridges. These are natural targets of interdiction for the American fighter-bombers, seeking to halt or slow down enemy supplies and reinforcements.

If a bridge is destroyed the Vietcong quickly re-route priority traffic and then construct a submerged span to replace the missing bridge. The new surface is just below water level, concealed by the swirling, muddy water, and is virtually invisible. Only reconnaissance shots that show traffic still using the road give a clue to the continued existence of a river crossing at that point. Another dodge is to build a pontoon bridge that carries traffic by night, and is swung aside and concealed by bankside trees or artificial camouflage by day.

Rail traffic is also important to the Vietcong, to bring in from China urgently needed ammunition and supplies. Needless to say, the railway wagons are extremely well camouflaged to avoid detection, often being completely 'thatched' by branches of trees and palm fronds.

Fortunately, the colour film that was introduced in Korea has proved most valuable in detecting such attempts at camouflage. In some instances, too, skilled interpretation of black and white photographs has shown that the Vietcong have made 'concealed' objects conspicuous by using as their cover-up material branches of trees not indigenous to the locality.

Bridges, vital mountain passes and airfields are of paramount importance to the Vietcong. To discourage attack they are surrounded by very heavy concentrations of anti-aircraft weapons, and their technique is to put up a vicious curtain of fire that any attacker must fly through. In the early days of the war in Vietnam the Americans tended to attack such targets on an unnecessarily regular basis, many individual targets being attacked again and again to prevent their use and to make re-construction impossible. This was a costly policy, in materials, machines and, most importantly, men.

High-altitude reconnaissance has stopped this wastage. Now a close watch is kept on, for example, an airfield that has been made unusable by bombing attack. When it is clear that repairs have been completed and the field is once again fit for operations, a new strike is made and the Vietcong are back at square one. This is a subtle system, for it has cost the enemy materials and tied up men who could have been employed on more aggressive tasks.

It may come as something of a surprise for British readers to learn that one of the aircraft responsible for this high-altitude watch is derived from the English Electric Canberra bomber. The RB–57F 'spy-plane' is an extensively-modified version of the licence-built Canberra. General Dynamics and Martin have been responsible for producing this machine, which has a wing almost double the span of the original as well as far more powerful engines. The result is an exceptional reconnaissance aircraft, which is reported to have a ceiling equal to, if not greater than, the U–2.

Perhaps the most vital task in Vietnam is the provision of tactical reconnaissance. Here the machine in the sky becomes the eyes of the ground commander, looking round the next bend, over the hill or into the jungle ahead. This means that the intelligence gained by the aircraft must be available quickly to the planner on the ground: no waiting 24 hours or more for photo-processing, when a decision to attack or withdraw must be made immediately.

One of the most sophisticated tools yet introduced to fill this important role is the USAF's RF–4C Phantom which has a maximum speed of Mach 2 plus. It carries optical, infra-red and electronic sensors, side- and forward-looking radar, and a battery of cameras which enable it to accomplish its role by day or night and in all weathers. To provide the 'instant' information needed by the units being assisted, an automatic in-flight film processing unit is installed and a special jettisonable cassette that can be ejected in flight. Within minutes of a photo sortie, the information can be in the hands of the commander on the ground, while UHF voice communications make it possible to amplify by description the photographic evidence.

By night the Phantom is just as valuable, but low-level missions over mountainous terrain would seem a more-than-dangerous task. Fortunately, this machine is equipped with terrain-following radar that feeds height and obstruction data to a computer which commands the autopilot, enabling the machine to fly safely at very low altitude. A pilot whose aircraft is following a course through a valley in pitch darkness needs a lot of faith in his equipment.

When peace talks were held in Paris in 1968, in an attempt to end the war in Vietnam, it came as something of a shock when the North Vietnamese Minister of State, Xuan Thuy, demanded as a prerequisite for any negotiations the cessation of all reconnaissance flights over his country.

Perhaps better than any other factor, this emphasises the valuable work of the reconnaissance units operating above the war-torn land of Vietnam. In this bitter and continuing struggle there seems no hint of an early peace. One can be certain only that when that happy moment arrives the 'eyes' in the sky will have played a major role—one in which they will have saved the lives of very many Americans and their allies.

# 10 ECM, AEW and ASW

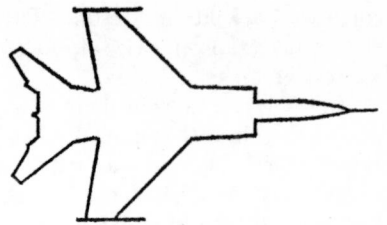

All seems peaceful at RAF Leuchars, in Scotland; but first impressions are deceptive. The two Lightning fighters of the Interception Alert Force, housed in a small, special hangar, are poised ready to go at any second, like highly-skilled athletes awaiting the starter's gun. Their fuel tanks are full, and the Red Top missiles clamped to each side of their fuselages are live and deadly.

Nor are the Lightnings' pilots as relaxed as they look, lounging in easy chairs, reading, watching television or playing cards as the hours tick by so very slowly. Even lunch had to be eaten inside heavy rubberised flying suits which can protect them against everything from the blood-draining agony of a tight turn at supersonic speed to a pressure-cabin failure ten miles high or a bail-out into a chilling winter sea.

Often, the whole day passes in boring inactivity. But not to-day.

Almost before a box on the wall has begun to squawk, magazines are flung aside and the pilots are dashing down the corridor towards their aircraft, pulling on Mae West lifejackets and buckling their flying suits as they go. No Battle of Britain 'scramble' was more professional, more hasty yet seeming unhurried, as the men are strapped into their cockpits and the hangar doors opened. No time-wasting taxying: the Lightnings were pointed down the runway as they waited. So they roar straight out of the hangar, down the concrete, with afterburners blazing, and begin that rocket-like climb to 30,000ft (9,150m) which no other fighter seems able to rival for sheer power and spectacle.

From the headphones built into his domed helmet, each pilot hears the calm voice of the ground controller, seated by a radar screen on the Aberdeenshire coast. Course is northeastward, at just below the speed of sound, with the grey waves of the North Sea far below.

While this scene of the drama has been enacted, the crew of a Tupolev Tu–95 bomber of the Soviet Naval Air Fleet have also been doing a job that is regarded as routine but could always end in sudden death and an international incident if they made a mistake. People sometimes regard electronic reconnaissance in peacetime as a sort of scientific matching of computer against computer, gadget against gadget, with men there only to ensure that the rules are not broken. This is a fallacy. The data ferreted out by electronics, cameras and other devices is needed for the serious business of preventing or waging a war that could eliminate all life over huge areas of the world, and the stakes in this game could not be higher.

The Russian aircrews have no illusions about catching the defences unprepared. Long ago, their aircraft first showed up as a 'blip' among the yellow lines and moving spots of light on a screen in the semi-darkness of a Norwegian radar station. Within seconds, the man watching the screen had been sufficiently certain of what he saw to reach for the telephone that alerted SHAPE Headquarters in Mons, Belgium, a USAF base near Reykjavik, Iceland, and RAF Strike Command Headquarters at High Wycombe in Buckinghamshire.

It was the decision of the duty air defence controller at High Wycombe that governed what happened next. The below-ground operations centre in which he works is the place from which the great offensive force of Bomber Command was controlled in World War II. Now, any one of the Vulcan jet-bombers listed on the huge board covering the wall in front of him could unleash greater destructive power than all the thousands of wartime Lancasters and Halifaxes added together; but today's operation calls for inspection by fighters rather than devastation by bombers—at least initially.

By now the intruder is being tracked on RAF radar screens in the north of Scotland, and by NATO observers in Europe. It is clearly heading through the Faroes gap, and the controller knows from all the data presented to him that the aircraft must be a giant Tu–95, loaded to the gunwales with intelligence sensors and known to NATO as 'Bear–D'. It was his reaction that launched the Lightnings from Leuchars.

Within minutes of crossing the Scottish coastline, their pilots see the 'Bear–D' straight ahead. Its pencil-thin fuselage bulges with radomes, aerials and blisters, inside which the very latest Russian equipment is hard at work, probing the radio and radar secrets of the NATO forces in Western Europe and the UK, trying to pinpoint the position of transmitters, learning their capability, seeking for gaps in their coverage. The crew of the big bomber feel no surprise as the Lightnings race towards them. Nor do they feel more than a moment's fear. Air forces usually play this game according to the rules and, being outside territorial limits, they feel safe, however menacing those Red Top missiles might look.

There was a time when RAF fighters could be shaken off by diving to a few feet above the wave-tops. At low altitude the Lightning's two big turbojets drank fuel at such a rate that it could only maintain its watchful escort for a short time before having to return to base. To-day, the same signal that alerted the Lightnings caused a Victor tanker-plane to take off from RAF Marham, in Norfolk. It is now standing off, a few miles away, ready to top up the fighters' tanks if the operation seems likely to last longer than an hour.

Flight refuelling in this way enables RAF fighters to fly out hundreds of miles to pick up Soviet ECM aircraft if necessary, and the Russian crews have no hope of giving their escort the slip. The Victor carries sufficient transfer fuel to keep a Lightning airborne for seventeen hours: a similar quantity of petrol would take the average family car three times round the world.

So, one of the observers inside a transparent blister under the 'Bear's' tailplane gives a wave to the nearest Lightning pilot that could be interpreted in any one of a dozen ways, from friendliness to a mocking 'can't touch me'. In feeling safe, he is luckier than some of the Americans who have performed similar intelligence-gathering flights around China, eastern Russia and other places for years.

Back in 1969, one such aircraft was cruising along off North Korea. It was a Lockheed EC–121M Constellation of the US Navy, bristling with reconnaissance equipment and carrying more than thirty men. One of the sensors they were operating enabled them not only to locate radars on the ground but to reproduce on their own screens, photograph and pass back to base exactly what the 'enemy' radar operator was seeing on his own screen at the same moment in time.

Like the crews of Russian 'Bears', and 'Badgers' that head round Norway, through the Faroes gap and down Britain's east coast, they had nothing to fear—in theory. But the North Korean MiGs that raced toward them did not waste time on friendly waves or the niceties of international law. With cannon blazing, they raked the unarmed Constellation until it crashed into the sea, with no survivors.

On April 18th 1969, President Nixon protested: "The mission was a reconnaissance which at no time took the plane closer to the shores of North Korea than 40 miles (64km). At the time the plane was shot down, all of the evidence we have indicates that it was approximately 90 miles (145km) from the shores of North Korea while it was moving outward, aborting the mission on orders that had been received. We knew this, based on our radar. What is even more important, the North Koreans knew it, based on their radar. Therefore, this attack was unprovoked. It was deliberate. It was without warning." The President might have added that it was by no means the only reconnaissance aircraft lost in similar circumstances in that part of the world.

However illegal, such actions are not surprising. The West has such immense capability in fashioning its own electronic defence systems and probing those of its potential enemies that the 'other side' cannot avoid being goaded into armed response occasionally. It is part of the price that has to be paid for the uneasy peace maintained by a deterrent threat of mutual, thermonuclear annihilation.

Few civilians appreciate the extent and efficiency of strategic reconnaissance in the 'seventies. The electronic 'ferrets' represent but one aspect of an immensely complex worldwide operation that involves small, unmanned drones, and satellites as big as a railway coach, as well as a great variety of aircraft. The equipment carried by the aeroplanes is so varied, for so many different purposes, that almost every photograph of EC–135 'spy-planes' operated by the USAF from bases in Japan seems to show a different, more puzzling permutation of bulges, radomes and antennae.

The public catches a brief, somewhat crude glimpse of one EC–135 capability when its TV screens carry pictures of Saturn/Apollo rocket vehicles blasting through space and staging, far beyond the range of ground cameras. Some of the other pictures acquired by EC–135s over the Pacific, on less publicised occasions, show equally fascinating shots of Soviet ICBMs scattering a pattern of inert MRV (multiple re-entry vehicle) warheads at the end of firing trials.

Such photographs convey little to an untrained observer. To the defence scientist, they might confirm whether the other side has yet progressed from a simple type of multiple warhead to one made up of separate charges which can manoeuvre independently to ensure greater accuracy or to elude the defences.

Nor do photographs represent the limit of vitally important data collected by the watching 'spy-planes'. For a decade, the US Department of Defense has conducted a research programme known by the acronym ABRES, at a cost of more than $1,000 million. The designation stands for Advanced Ballistic Re-Entry System; its aim is to develop the means for American land-based and submarine-based ballistic missiles to penetrate constantly improving enemy area and point defence systems with adequate accuracy and large enough payloads to ensure the destruction of a variety of targets.

ABRES seeks to discover the best shape for warhead re-entry vehicles and the best method of shielding them from the intense heat built up as they re-enter the Earth's atmosphere from space. At one time it was sufficient to prove that the vehicles *could* survive re-entry and would not topple or yaw so much that the accuracy of their trajectory was affected. Now the main warheads must be accompanied by decoys, protected by ECM devices, and made rugged enough to survive nuclear blasts from enemy ABMs (anti-ballistic missiles) and the stresses imposed by manoeuvring, as well as the intense heat inseparable from any re-entry.

The decoys have to produce the same 'blip' on a radar screen as one of the warheads if they are to be effective. This is not helped by the fact that any object re-entering the atmosphere trails an 'ionised wake' which, by its nature, can give enemy radar observers positive information on the mass and other aspects of the body. It is, therefore, essential to modify the wake created by decoys if they are to be credible.

America's ABRES programme is concerned with these and other aspects of the nation's own ballistic missiles. As part of its extensive network of facilities, it utilises two specially-modified KC–135 aircraft known by the acronym TRAP, for Terminal Radiation Airborne measurements Programme. What lies inside the hump on the back of each aircraft, behind the rows of special windows down the sides of its fuselage and inside other fairings is known only to the security-bound men who service, fly and control the aircraft. But remarkable photographs have been published showing re-entering warheads; and radiation data collected by the KC–135s is helping to keep America's ICBMs at least one big step ahead of their Soviet counterparts, which are under continuous observation by other C–135s (under programmes like the USAF's Cobra Ball) and surface ships.

Such missions help to keep track of the opposition's progress in weapon development. They give no clue to how the US President is able to say, as he did on February 9th 1972: "There is evidence that two new or greatly modified (Soviet) ICBM systems are being developed. Nearly 100 new ICBM sites are being constructed. Some of these silos are for large, modern missiles such as the SS–9 which, because of their warhead size and potential accuracy, could directly threaten our land-based ICBMs. . . . An improved submarine-launched ballistic missile is also being perfected. . . . A new Soviet bomber is being flight-tested. ABM (anti-ballistic missile system) construction has been resumed around Moscow; new types of ABM radars and ballistic missile interceptor systems are being tested."

Such comprehensive knowledge of Russia's top-secret military research and deployment must owe much to America's reconnaissance satellites, described in the last chapter of this book. But there is another side to the picture.

When a city in the north-east US was about to open a fine new museum, its staff thought that it would be interesting to include a picture of the biggest possible area around their city, taken from a satellite. Enquiries to NASA and the Department of Defense elicited replies that such pictures could never be made available to civilian organisations, as they must inevitably show secret installations such as airfields and missile sites.

Tongue-in-cheek, the curator next dropped a line to Moscow, with a similar request. It was received by somebody who had either a sense of humour or a better-than-average understanding of the modern deterrent. So, the American museum can now display the space photo it wanted, by courtesy of a Soviet satellite which had no inhibitions about recording the area—military sites and all!

Precise data on what modern strategic reconnaissance can achieve are not often published. Before switching to tactical recce, it might therefore be worthwhile recording one aspect of the capability of the Victor B(SR)2 reconnaissance aircraft operated by No 543 Squadron from RAF Wyton in Huntingdonshire. Here is an aircraft mighty enough and complex enough to dash out to the Mediterranean, at heights far above that at which the airlines fly, and radar-map the whole of that vast area, by itself, in a single seven-hour sortie by day or night. So good are the resulting prints that the position of every ship at sea or in harbour can be pinpointed.

How good, one wonders, are the results achieved by the Russian 'Bears' and Tu–16 'Badgers', the supersonic Tu–22 'Blinders', the Il–38 'Moss' maritime reconnaissance bombers based on the Il–18 turboprop airliner, and the Be–12 'Mail' amphibians which shadow, photograph and 'listen' electronically to NATO fleets at sea, in every ocean? Not until such aircraft, or satellites, can guarantee to detect and pinpoint every missile-carrying submarine hiding in the seas will the East–West deterrent lose any of its terrible viability.

Aircraft built for anti-submarine warfare (ASW) operations are among the most security-wrapped types used by air forces today. Even a trusted visitor who walks through a Nimrod MR 1 of No 201 Squadron of the RAF at Kinloss, in Scotland, is likely to find covers over some of the displays on the starboard side of its tactical compartment. This is understandable, as no other ASW aircraft is so well equipped to track down and destroy the underwater craft that hold the key to survival of half the world in their missile launch-tubes.

Four Rolls-Royce Spey turbofan engines give the Nimrod the ability to dash out to a patrol area at up to 575mph (925km/h). Two of the engines can be shut down to conserve fuel during the seemingly endless periods of searching vast areas of ocean. At any moment, during a reconnaissance lasting twelve hours, a submarine might be detected by radar, one of the sonar systems, the Autolycus ionisation detector which sniffs the trail left in the water by a submerged craft, or one of the other search devices. Immediately the pilot will turn the big 80-ton aircraft towards its potential prey, opening the 50ft- (15.25m) long weapon bay doors to reveal a variety of bombs, depth charges and homing torpedoes that are supplemented by air-to-surface missiles under the wings. This is Nimrod, named so very appropriately after the 'mighty hunter before the Lord' in the Bible's book of Genesis.

No carrier-based aircraft is large enough to carry all of the equipment and weapons packed aboard the Nimrod; but the US Navy's new S–3A Viking gives a good idea of the degree of efficiency that such aircraft can attain. Let us imagine we are on board a Viking which has just entered operational service on the huge nuclear-powered carrier *Enterprise*, in 1974.

Unlike the heavily-laden fighters and strike aircraft, there is no need for our aeroplane to latch on to a steam catapult and be flung violently into the air. A deck more than 1,000ft (305m) long, heading into wind at 30 knots, enables it to make a gentle take-off more suited to a pleasure flight than to the deadly serious business of sub-hunting.

To-day is a practice mission, and we have the satisfaction of knowing that there is a submarine in a specified vast area of the Pacific Ocean over which we are flying. Let us be honest, and admit right away that the task of searching for the proverbial needle in a haystack would be simple compared with trying to find a missile-carrying submarine that might be anywhere in the waters that cover seven-tenths of the Earth's surface.

Side-by-side on the flight deck are the pilot and co-pilot. The pilot is no longer at the controls. Since shortly after take-off he has left the flying to a computerised automatic flight-control system which can do the job with unrivalled efficiency, leaving him free to concentrate on the tactical situation. The main computer does the work of a whole plane-load of men, storing and recalling data from all the sensors carried by the aircraft, monitoring the electronics for malfunctions and increasing the accuracy of tactical manoeuvres.

On his cathode-ray tube (CRT) the pilot is given full data on fly-to points, time, aircraft position and track, 'fixes' and predicted target positions. He receives automatic cues and alerts, recommended sequences of action and data on the positions of sonobuoys that have been dropped to investigate any sector of ocean that might be hiding a submarine.

In the right-hand seat, the co-pilot must not only be prepared to take over the controls at any moment but is also responsible for navigation, communications and operating the whole range of non-acoustic sensors, such as radar, the magnetic anomaly detector in the Viking's MAD 'tail-sting', forward-looking infra-red and ECM.

Any suspicious 'blip' that shows up on the co-pilot's CRT can be encircled by moving an electronic marker across the face of the screen. A push-button will then feed the 'contact' into the computer, make it available on the displays of the other crew-members, and even pass it by data-link to operators in other aircraft or surface ships. All emergencies are provided for. The navigation and communications duties of the co-pilot can be taken over by other crew-members, whose own tasks can, equally, be passed on or shared.

In a completely enclosed cabin behind the Viking's flight deck sit the Sensor Operator (Senso) and Tactical Co-ordinator (Tacco). The latter directs the entire sub-hunting mission, following the changing tactical situation on his CRT, viewing the data from all the aircraft's sensors, assessing it and issuing instructions to the other crew-members. The Senso is primarily responsible for operation of the acoustic data systems, but can back up the pilot's monitoring of non-acoustic sensors.

Careful training, and the availability of automatic target-detection and computer-aided classification of contacts, make every Viking sortie a thoroughly professional counter to the most elusive, formidable weapons system known to man. As the aircraft flies its pre-determined track at a search speed of around 185mph (300km/h), the radar in its nose spins and scans the water continuously, able to detect even small targets in a rough sea. From a retractable turret in the belly, further aft, an infra-red sensor —aimed automatically by the computer—ensures high-quality resolution of a target by day or night, being independent of ambient illumination and able to penetrate haze and light fog. Two sets of lenses provide wide-angle or 'zoom' presentation and, once detected, a target is tracked automatically, ensuring that it will never be lost even if it moves temporarily from the crew's field of view.

A fuselage-mounted KB–18A panoramic camera provides horizon-to-horizon surveillance coverage, and is available to record the results of any attack. The MAD (magnetic anomaly detection) 'sting' projecting from the aircraft's tail searches for metallic objects beneath the surface, reporting any anomaly in the magnetic field that might indicate the presence of a submarine. And all the time ECM pods at the wingtips are ready to pick up the faintest signals which might suggest that a submarine is receiving radar warning of the Viking's approach; so that the enemy's signals can be jammed and data provided to the computer that will enable it to swing the aircraft on a homing course towards the radar transmitter.

Sixty sonobuoys are stored in chutes in the rear fuselage. Dropped singly, or in patterns, they 'listen' for the sound emissions that come from even the latest quiet submarines, pinpointing the position of the target. The computer absorbs all the resulting data and can handle both the manoeuvring of the aircraft into the attack position and the selection and dropping of depth bombs and destructors, or the firing of rockets.

In fact, on this occasion, the target has been found and 'destroyed' in a simulated attack that we might well have missed had not the pilot drawn our attention to the various stages of the operation on his CRT. Such is the degree of automation achieved with even a relatively small modern ASW aircraft.

Meanwhile, the tactical reconnaissance task which was handled so easily by the 90mph (145km/h) wood-and-canvas biplanes of 1914–18 now employs a vast range of widely-diversant types, costing billions of pounds, dollars, roubles and any other currency one cares to name.

Having eliminated, perhaps for all time, the threat of a third and entirely-final World War, the so-called 'powers' have degenerated into participation in campaigns variously referred to as limited, local, 'brushfire', counter-insurgency or some other term that covers semi-legalised killing of fellow human beings. As always, this can be done economically only by knowing as much as possible about the other side.

With such campaigns limited so far to the use of non-nuclear weapons, it has usually been possible to develop tactical reconnaissance aircraft as conversions of existing designs. Except in the case of a few very specialised types, it has even been practicable to retain much of the offensive or defensive capability of aircraft which began as combat machines.

Thus, a high proportion of modern fighters, such as the American F–4 Phantom and F–5, the French Mirage III and the Swedish Draken, can be produced as competent tactical reconnaissance aircraft by fitting a new fuselage nose containing automatic cameras.

In some cases, an even simpler installation can be utilised, in the form of a reconnaissance pod carried on one of the aircraft's external weapon racks. A particularly good example of such a pod is that developed by EMI Electronics for carriage by Phantoms of the Royal Air Force. Carried on the underfuselage weapon pylon, it contains cameras and EMI's Type P331 side-looking radar, which uses the linescan system to record on 12.7cm film a radar map of the terrain to each side of the aircraft's flight path. In this way, the Phantom can combine first-class reconnaissance equipment with Mach 2 performance and a heavy load of missiles or other weapons.

The RAF's Harrier goes one big stage further for straightforward battle-field recce, being able to take off and land vertically, without needing easily-damaged runways. It packs a nose camera as standard equipment, can carry a five-camera pack under its fuselage, and is unrivalled in combining the go-anywhere versatility of a helicopter with the transonic performance expected in a modern strike aircraft.

In every respect, including cost, the Harrier is a first-class aeroplane for first-class air forces which might get involved in a major war. Since 1945, the world's aircraft industries have been trying to find a formula for a relatively simple, inexpensive, multi-purpose combat machine tailored to the smaller wars that seem to have become inevitable. They have achieved little success, mainly because the major powers are too ready to pour into countries like Vietnam and Egypt the kind of weapons and electronic defence systems that can be offset only by the most advanced and fully-equipped aircraft.

This is why the USAF found itself committed to using the F–105D Thunderchief as the spearhead of its attack force in the years when it pounded targets in North Vietnam ceaselessly. By World War II standards, only a modest number of F–105Ds had been built (something over 600). They cost more than $2 million each, and were lost at a rate that was not only unjustified but threatened to reduce to a dangerous level the number of hard-hitting fighter-bombers available to the USAF in its primary task of confronting the Communist powers in Europe and the Far East.

To reduce the demands being made on primary combat aircraft, needed elsewhere, the US Services began adapting older types for tasks that could be undertaken comparatively safely with a minimum of expensive equipment. Hence the forward air controllers in Bird Dogs, seeking out and marking targets for fighter-bomber attacks in southern Vietnam, far away from the missiles and radar-controlled anti-aircraft guns that defended the North; and the old C–47 (Dakota) and C–119 piston-engined transports modified into gunships for night attacks on Vietcong and North Vietnamese insurgents.

Successes achieved by the 'Spooky' and 'Shadow' gunships, and the little Bird Dogs, persuaded the US Navy and USAF that it would be worthwhile investigating the usefulness of a relatively small and inexpensive, entirely-new, combat aircraft tailored especially for modern counter-insurgency operations. The result, after several years of design, development and evaluation, was the North American Rockwell OV–10 Bronco.

Powered by two 715hp turboprops, this twin-boomed two-seater has plank-like wings and tailplane of the kind described as being made by the mile and cut off by the yard. Its bulbous cockpit canopy gives a superb all-round view while its crew search for the brief flash of movement that might betray a handful of guerrillas in a jungle clearing. Its top speed of 281mph (452km/h) and range of a few hundred miles are adequate for its tasks. Furthermore, it is well equipped to defend itself against the kind of enemy it seeks. Four machine-guns are fitted inside sponsons that protrude on each side of its fuselage; and racks under the sponsons, fuselage and wings can haul a ton and a half of bombs, rockets, napalm and air-to-air missiles.

(Left) Launch of Tiros, the American satellite which pointed the way to modern reconnaissance 'spies in the sky'.

(Right) This photograph of a Midas ballistic missile warning satellite was released before such pictures were banned for security reasons. /USAF

The technique by which reconnaissance satellites are recovered is illustrated by this picture of the 'air-snatch' of a Discoverer satellite. The JC–130B Hercules aircraft was despatched from Hickam Air Force Base, Hawaii.

Cameras about to be loaded on to a Victor B(SR) Mk 2 strategic reconnaissance aircraft of No 543 Squadron at RAF Wyton.

...ew of the vast range of Teledyne Ryan Remotely Piloted Vehicles (RPVs) with their
...–130A launch aircraft and recovery helicopters. Included are a supersonic Firebee II
...eground), Models 154 and 147 (second row), and a Model 234 and two Model 147s
...rd row).

...del 147 RPV suspended from the wing pylon of a DC–130A. Thirteen 'hashmarks' on
...uselage denote missions already completed.

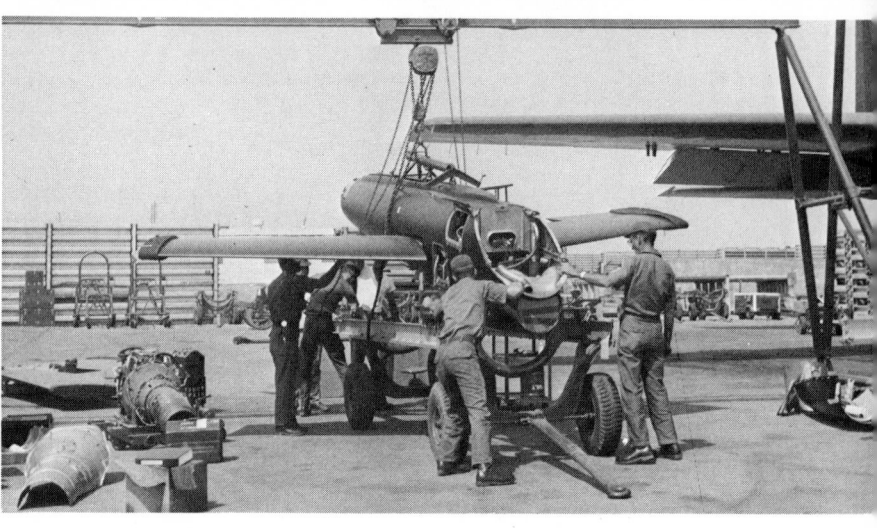

(Above) The large size of Teledyne Ryan's Model 154 RPVs is emphasised by this photograph of two of them under the wings of a DC–130A launch/director aircraft, which spans 132ft 7in.

(Top) Top-secret devices packed on board the RPVs result in some strange profiles. This is yet another variation of the basic Model 147.

(Top left) Preparing a drone for an unspecified mission on behalf of USAF Tactical Air Command.

(Centre left) Refurbishing a Model 147 RPV followed an operational mission. Its baby turbojet engine is shown, on the ground, under the starboard wingtip.

(Left) Model 154 RPV recovered by a Sikorsky HH–3E helicopter, which snagged its recovery parachute in mid-air. The small drogue chute stabilises the drone in flight under the helicopter.

(Left) Remarkable photographs are brought back by
reconnaissance RPVs. This
one was taken from a drone
which passed safely between
two pylons, under power
cables, during a mission
over North Vietnam.

(Right) Cape Kennedy
photographed with a handheld Hasselblad camera
from the orbiting Gemini 4
spacecraft in June 1965.
/NASA

(Left) Also taken by a drone
over North Vietnam was
this photograph of a
camouflaged anti-aircraft
gun site.

(Right) This photograph of
the state of Nevada, taken
from the Apollo 9 spacecraft
in March 1969, gives some
indication of the high
standard of detail that can
be obtained from an altitude
of well over 100 miles.
/NASA

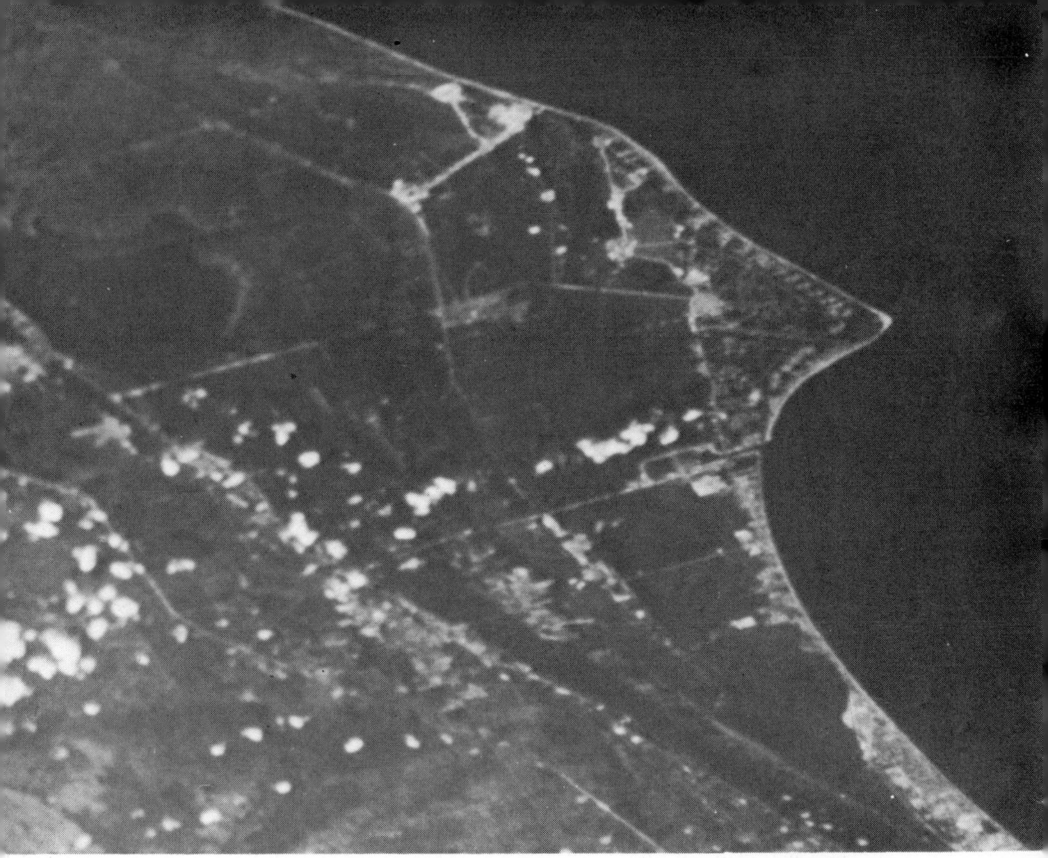

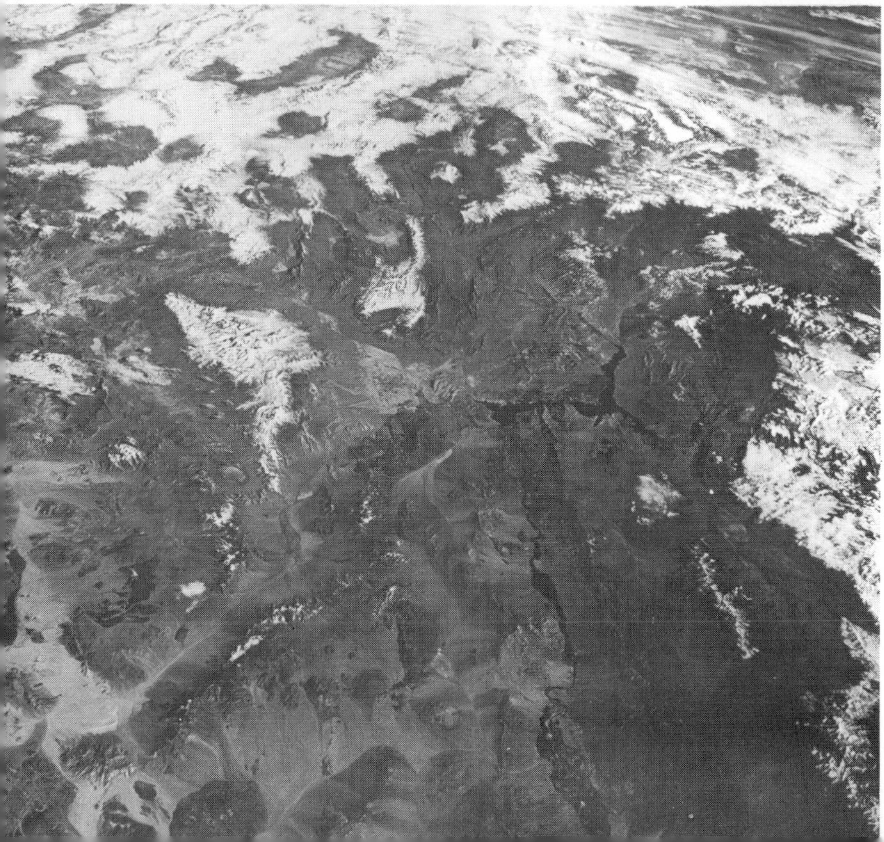

Full-size replica of the first orbital space station, made up of the Soyuz 4 and Soyuz 5 spacecraft, on display in the Soviet Economic Achievements Exhibition, Moscow. /Tass

Mouth of the Colorado River in northern Baja California, photographed from the Apollo 9 spacecraft at a height of 150 miles, using colour infra-red film. /NASA

Despite such apparent attractions and the early success of the Bronco in Vietnam, the USAF ordered only 152, with another 96 going to the US Marine Corps. Even guerrillas, travelling on foot in jungle terrain, can muster such heavy fire-power, and 'disappear' so effectively when they wish, that the unsophisticated counter-insurgency aircraft has severe limitations.

Nothing illustrates this better than the fact that experience in Vietnam dictated an expenditure of $2,500 million on electronic warfare by the American services between 1965 and 1970. Even with US withdrawal from the war well advanced in 1972, the US Navy alone decided to spend a further $250 million that year on electronic warfare equipment for its Phantom, Skyhawk, Vigilante, Intruder and Corsair II aircraft.

Even the outward and visible results of such huge investment are impressive. Still-secret developments, reserved for last-ditch necessity in a major East–West confrontation, would read like the pages of some barely-credible science-fiction prophesy of the far future.

Reconnaissance, in its many forms, has become interwoven so inextricably with the military duties of electronic intelligence (elint) gathering, airborne early warning (AEW), electronic countermeasures (ECM), electronic counter-countermeasures (ECCM), airborne warning and control system (AWACS) operations, anti-submarine warfare (ASW) and other tasks that the aeroplane itself is the least complex and least costly component of the overall weapon system.

The code names by which the different systems are designated by the US Services make James Bond seem dully Victorian and lacking in imagination. The USAF can contribute Black Crow, Combat Angel, Compass Dawn, Comfy Bee, Commando Bolt, Compass Cope, Compass Dwell, Compass Ghost, Compass Quick, Have Fault, Have Lemon, Have Orchid, Pave Eagle, and half a hundred others. The US Navy adds Blue Charger, ERASE, Hip Pocket, See Saw, Tree Cat and other systems of which even the code-names are restricted. The US Army offers Quick Look, Quick Fix, Cefirm Leader and Cefirm Scavenger. To Soviet and Chinese radars, NATO applies an equally fascinating selection of codes such as Puff Ball, Short Horn, Skip Spin, High Fix, Long Talk, One Eye, Two Spot, Crosslegs, Squat Eye, Moon Cone and Tall King.

In every corner of the globe these electronic eyes, ears and voices are in action, all day, every day—deterring, spying, helping some men to kill and helping whole continents to stay alive.

As this book is being written, there are little twin-engined US Army Beechcraft RU–21s over Vietnam, not very different from the King Airs that carry businessmen between board meetings. The main difference is that these particular aircraft look as if they hit the airfield boundary fence on take-off and have carried some of the posts impaled on their wings and tail. These are the kind of machines used for Cefirm missions, locating and jamming the enemy's communications and cracking his codes.

Not all missions require aircraft to be stationed in or near the area that is being watched or jammed. One of America's most successful electronic warfare programmes has been Igloo White, which requires aircraft only to set up the surveillance system and then to deal with targets that it locates.

Igloo White was made necessary by the unique nature of the Vietnam War. Most of the enemy's supplies of arms and equipment came from Russia and China, notably through the port of Haiphong. This was off-limits for attack for years, which meant that the most vulnerable portion of the enemy's supply lines was that section of the Ho Chi Minh Trail which ran through Laos. There could be few more difficult targets. Any road or bridge that was made impassable by bombing could quickly be by-passed by one or other of the network of interconnected roads, hidden for the most part under a jungle canopy. And the kind of limited, small-unit operations conducted in the south made it difficult to detect and attack the spasmodic convoys of trucks used to keep the combat units in action.

Hence Igloo White, which utilises three main elements: sensors of various types which are 'sown' by aircraft along carefully selected stretches of the Ho Chi Minh Trail; an orbiting aircraft which picks up signals from these sensors when they detect enemy traffic and passes on the information to the third element; an Infiltration Surveillance Center (ISC), built in 1968, where the information is processed by computer and analysed by officers who can call up an immediate air strike if this is considered worthwhile.

A typical sequence of events begins with the dispatch of a formation of F–4 Phantom fighter-bombers, each carrying a number of sensor dispensers under its wings. Over the chosen sector of the infiltration route these sensors are released in a carefully-planned pattern. They are of four basic kinds. The 66in- (167cm) long Spikebuoy is a 40lb (18kg) acoustic sensor, derived from the naval sonobuoy, which buries itself in the ground when dropped, leaving only its antenna exposed. Its microphone, powered by a long-life battery, then begins listening for passing traffic and other activity. The camouflaged Acoubuoy, 36in (91cm) long, is similar except that it is designed to parachute into trees or jungle where it can hang and do its work.

Adsid (Air Delivered Seismic Detection Sensor) has been used even more widely. Only 33in (84cm) long, it is shaped like a dart, and buries itself in the ground leaving only its twig-like antenna showing. It is sensitive enough to pick up the ground vibrations caused by moving traffic and has the big advantage of using far less power than the acoustic sensors, so that it offers a much longer service life. This is important, as even an Adsid costs $975 and the complete Igloo White project had absorbed $725 million by mid-1971.

Fourth kind of sensor is Acousid, which can transmit both sound and seismic data. Like the others, it passes the information to an orbiting relay aircraft for onward transmission to the ISC. Most widely used relay has been the EC–121R version of the Constellation transport, which offered the advantage of accommodating a large crew to monitor the data and call up a strike force in advance of ISC action if such urgent response seemed essential. Disadvantages were the high cost of the EC–121R and the vulnerability of such a large, slowly-orbiting aircraft. Consequently, Project Pave Eagle was devised to replace the Constellations with small, relatively inexpensive relay aircraft based on 'off-the-shelf' types like the Beech Bonanza lightplane, which could be flown either manually or by remote control as pilotless drones. The QU–22B version of the Bonanza is fitted, for this task, with a 376hp Continental GTSIO–520 engine, driving a three-blade, large-diameter Hartzell propeller which is geared to turn slowly and quietly.

Let us assume that an Adsid has reported movement of a truck convoy, via an orbiting QU–22B to the ISC. An immediate strike is clearly worthwhile, so a squadron of F–4 Phantom II fighter-bombers is directed to the target area, where a Forward Air Controller (FAC) waits in an O–2A to direct the attack. Unfortunately, the ground fire is too hot this time to permit the O–2A to stay in the area. It does not matter. The pilots of the Phantoms feed into their airborne computers the target co-ordinates supplied by the Adsids. The computers then take over navigation to the target and release automatically the heavy loads of fragmentation bombs so that they will arrive at an aiming point on the Ho Chi Minh Trail simultaneously with the convoy of enemy trucks.

If it were night-time, the Phantoms would probably be replaced by big AC–119 or AC–130 gunship transports, able to pour the concentrated fire of a battery of multi-barrel guns into the target area. At one time, night movement was far safer for the enemy than daytime operation under the watchful eyes of the FAC and the never-far-off fighter-bombers. The gunships changed all this, using infra-red and other sensors to locate their targets before opening up with their guns.

Even the big B–52 Stratofortress bombers joined in Igloo White, carpeting with every kind of non-nuclear bomb places that had been pinpointed as daytime parking areas for trucks. Special weapons, as well as special sensors and specially-equipped aircraft, have all played their part, including extremely accurate 'smart bombs' like Hobos (Homing Bomb System), guided to their targets by laser or electro-optical devices.

Such developments account for many of the strange-sounding USAF code names. Black Crow, for example, is a sensor fitted to AC–130 gunships that can detect the ignition system of a truck engine. Commando Bolt covers all-weather blind-bombing strikes by high-speed aircraft like Phantoms against targets located by Igloo White sensors; and Have Fault is a personnel detector.

Between them, all these applications of advanced technology helped to raise the number of enemy trucks destroyed on the Ho Chi Minh Trail from 5,950 between November 1969 and April 1970 to about 14,000 in the same period of 1970–71. Without the surveillance by Igloo White, little of this success would have been possible.

Vietnam is not, by any means, the only area of interest. On a course parallel to the border of one of the Warsaw Pact countries in Europe, another US Army 'spy-plane', an OV–1D Mohawk, is cruising along at a sedate 200mph (320km/h). There is a cigar-shape Motorola side-looking radar clamped under its belly, a camera and photoflash pod, a Sylvania fuse jammer under its port wingtip and a Hallicrafters radar noise jammer under its starboard wingtip to protect it from Russian 'Guideline' surface-to-air missiles, and an Itek radar warning system whose wingtip and tail antennae signal the approach of hostile fighters. Aircraft of this basic type perform the Army's Quick Look missions, flying just outside enemy airspace to 'ferret' out elint data on surface-to-air missile systems.

From a US Navy carrier, stationed off Hué, a strike force of A–6 Intruders heads towards a North Vietnamese armoured column that has crossed the demilitarised zone. Most of the aircraft are two-seat A–6As, bristling with weapons; at their head is a solitary four-seat EA–6B, without which they might never penetrate the defences to hit their targets.

The capabilities of modern anti-aircraft missiles were demonstrated dramatically years ago, when the US Navy cruiser *Long Beach*, in the waters off Vietnam, picked up a pair of enemy MiGs more than 70 miles (112km) away. The fighter pilots felt perfectly safe, over friendly territory, and with no hostile air activity showing on ground radars. Without warning, both MiGs were suddenly hit and destroyed by Talos missiles launched from the ship their pilots never saw.

'Guidelines' lack the range of Talos but are still to be treated with respect. Hence the vital importance of the unarmed EA–6B. Under its wings and fuselage are the five pods of an ALQ–99 tactical noise jamming system, each containing two transmitters. On the tip of its tail-fin is an ugly pod containing the ALQ–99 receivers and six antennae. Beneath it, on the sides of the fin, are ECM receiver antennae. Another antenna, thrusting forward from one of the pylons under its port wing, is part of an ALQ–100 deception ECM (DECM) system which makes enemy radars report false directional data if the jammers fail to blot them out entirely.

These systems are the kind that are being updated under Blue Charger for installation on the very latest Navy combat aircraft, including the F–14 Tomcat 'swing-wing' fighter. When this Mach 2+ design begins its prowl in search of prey, it will have many other tricks up its feline sleeve, including a pair of ALE–29B dispensers which fling out chaff (what used to be called Window) and flares to confuse enemy radars and attract infra-red homing missiles to where they cannot harm the Tomcat.

Decoys are not new. A decade ago, B–52 bombers of the USAF Strategic Air Command could launch tiny jet-powered, winged Quails from their bomb bay, to tear around the sky for hundreds of miles, on a predetermined course at the same speed as the B–52, each giving the same 'blip' on enemy radar screens as the mighty eight-engined bomber from which it came. Today's decoys are smaller and more subtle, like the tiny ECM pods which can be scattered from fighters to descend under foldable parawings and jam enemy radars for periods up to half an hour.

As the US Navy Intruders return to their carrier off Vietnam, the ship is guarded by an E–2 Hawkeye, flying in lazy circles that bely the hive of activity inside it. Up to now, enemy aircraft have tended to ignore the huge, tempting naval targets from which endless air strikes have been launched; but this offers no excuse for relaxed vigilance. In an era of deadly anti-shipping missiles which can travel at wave-top height, below the cover of ship-borne radar, and home on their target at supersonic speed, everything approaching the carrier must be detected and tracked.

Above the Hawkeye's fuselage, a big radar scanner spins inside its huge saucer-shape fairing. Already it has picked up the Intruders. If the enemy tried to slip in a flight of attack aircraft under cover of the returning strike, the Hawkeye's radar observers could not only give warning but, if necessary, provide full guidance for US Navy interceptors to deal with the threat.

Such are the duties of an AWACS (airborne warning and control system) aircraft. The Hawkeye is not alone in this category. If Alexei Khrunov's MiG–23 squadron, in Egypt, had ever flown into action to repel an Israeli attack, its aircrew would have been alerted and directed by a giant turbo-prop aircraft known to NATO as 'Moss'. Based on the Tu–114 transport, with an endurance of more than half a day, its saucer radome and other antennae can provide all the information needed by MiG–23s to attack a strike force flying at supersonic speed at any altitude.

Never again will combat aeroplanes be the simple, uncluttered shapes they used to be. Reconnaissance—the vital key to victory on land and sea that gave birth to military aviation—has proliferated to such a degree that it must now dominate military thinking, planning and spending. 'Know your enemy' is the oldest of old axioms for the war leader. Equally, the enemy must be prevented from knowing you.

The pilot of a USAF F–4D Phantom has little time to ponder such thoughts as he crosses the demilitarised zone north of Quangtri. Under his wing is a pod containing a computer-controlled radar homing, warning and avoidance system known as Wild Weasel. The pilot may not realise that the radars of a North Vietnamese 'Guideline' missile site have locked on to him; but Wild Weasel does. It feeds data to the Phantom's fire control system which, at the right moment, launches an air-to-surface missile named Standard ARM. The acronym stands for Anti-Radiation Missile.

Before the enemy missile-men realise what is happening and have time to switch off their radar, Standard ARM has locked on to it and is on a collision course at supersonic speed. The men will die because they happen to be around; the real fight is between electronic devices that can do everything but reason why.

# 11 Blackbirds and Peewits

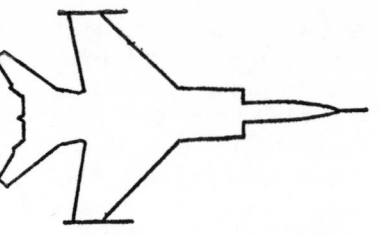

The man has not quite been superseded by the computer. His small, living brain remains the most accurate, most reliable, compact control unit in existence. It is the only one that can make decisions based on a peculiar human blend of reason, experience, circumstance and caution. Unfortunately, the package in which it is wrapped was not designed to withstand the strains and stresses of a supersonic, atomic, electronic age.

So, when a pair of human brains need to be plugged into a mechanical masterpiece of the 'seventies, like one of the Blackbirds of Beale, the vehicles of flesh and blood in which they have the misfortune to function must be checked for efficiency and then coddled for survival.

For the benefit of the uninitiated, it should be explained that the Blackbirds are Lockheed SR–71A aircraft. Beale is the name of the US Air Force base in California that houses the 9th Strategic Reconnaissance Wing to which they belong.

When President Johnson first revealed the existence of these aircraft, on February 29th 1964, he said that they had already been tested in sustained flight at speeds of more than 2,000mph (3,200km/h) and at heights in excess of 70,000ft (21,350m). This far exceeded the world absolute speed record, which then stood at 1,665.9mph (2,681km/h), set by a Russian research aircraft. Any temptation toward scepticism passed quickly when it was learned that the new aircraft, known by the designation A–11, was a product of the same 'Skunk Works' at Burbank that had earlier developed the U–2.

Four years had passed since the Powers affair, and the President stressed that the A–11 was being tested as a potential long-range fighter, with the service designation YF–12A. Nobody doubted, however, that the original intention had been to evolve a successor to the U–2—even if overflights of the Soviet Union were abandoned after 1960. So it caused no surprise when the President announced, on July 24th 1964, that Lockheed was developing a second Mach 3 aircraft, designated SR–71, as 'a long-range advanced strategic reconnaissance plane, capable of worldwide reconnaissance for military operations' and equipped with multiple sensors.

When photographs of the SR–71A were released, it was clearly a variant of the same basic A–11 design as the YF–12A. A clue to its capability came on May Day 1965—exactly five years after Gary Powers' U–2 had been shot down—when YF–12As smashed three world records and six class records. These included an absolute speed record of 2,070.102mph (3,331.507 km/h) over a 15/25km course, and a sustained height record of 80,258ft (24,462m) in horizontal flight, neither of which has since been beaten.

Nothing like the SR–71A had ever before been seen in military service when deliveries began in January 1966. Its needle-nose fuselage is 107ft 5in (32.74m) long; its delta wings span 55ft 7in (16.95m); and it weighs about 170,000lb (77,110kg), which is far more than the loaded weight of a Trident airliner carrying 180 passengers. Construction is almost entirely of titanium, as conventional aviation metals would melt at three times the speed of sound. Yet this, and more, is the *cruising* speed of the SR–71A, at which it can cover nearly 3,000 miles (4,800km) at a height of 78,750ft (24,000m).

Although reluctant to say too much about its hottest aircraft, the USAF has commented that equipment carried internally ranges from simple battlefield surveillance systems to multiple-sensor high-performance systems for interdiction reconnaissance and strategic systems capable of specialised surveillance of up to 60,000 square miles (155,400km$^2$) of territory in one hour.

This is the kind of aeroplane that most youngsters dream of flying. Few make it, for a succession of very good reasons. Something of what it takes to be chosen to pilot an SR–71 has been told by Lt-Col G. Abe Kardong,* who has been with the Blackbird programme since 1967, as an SR–71 pilot and Chief of SR–71 Crew Training and Protocol.

When the USAF first began recruiting crews for the programme, the prerequisites were set out quite simply: "Pilots must have 1,500 hours of jet time, be a volunteer, under thirty-five years of age, and physically qualified". In fact, the average man chosen back in the mid-sixties was aged thirty-five, had started his career with a tour on fighters, progressed to Strategic Air Command service on B–58s, B–52s, or U–2s, logged some 3,800 flying hours and earned a high OER (officers' evaluation report) rating. Most of them are now lieutenant colonels. The 'youngsters' who took their place are normally captains or majors, aged thirty-one, with 2,500 flying hours in their log-books, including a fighter tour in South-East Asia.

Behind each pilot, in the SR–71's rear seat, is a reconnaissance systems officer (RSO) of captain rank, aged about thirty, with experience as a radar navigator on B–52s or B–58s, a total of 2,500 flying hours and a first-class physical rating.

Thirty may be pushing it age-wise for a pop idol, but things happen fast in a Blackbird, and there's no substitute for experience. For example, one of the aircraft's little tricks, which does not happen so often now, was christened the 'inlet restart'.

To understand precisely what this means requires a fair technical knowledge. Skipping the technicalities, it is sufficient to know that a

* *High, Hot and Headin' Out* (Air Force Magazine, December 1971).

complex set of engine air intake controls (including the centre-body 'spike') is needed to keep the supersonic shock-wave positioned precisely in the engine inlet. Most supersonic aircraft are designed to keep the shock-wave outside the intake duct; the SR–71 'swallows' it. At high supersonic speeds, each engine by-passes the majority of the high-speed airflow around the compressor; this air is, however, compressed by the inlet and ejected from the rear of the engine. In other words, the engine functions as a kind of air pump, with a high proportion of the total thrust being produced by the inlet itself.

This is fine for most of the time. Unfortunately, any one of a variety of malfunctions can cause the shock-wave to be expelled from the inlet throat. When this happens, according to Colonel Kardong: "With a sudden loss of most of the thrust, the aircraft attempts to 'swap ends' at high supersonic speeds. This violent, mind-boggling experience has been described as like having a mid-air collision. Until the inlet is 'restarted', the pilot's head is sometimes bounced from one side of the canopy to the other, and his eyeballs touch all their limit switches. With the advent of automatic restart systems, this situation is now very rare. The possibility of its happening, however, tends to keep the crew alert."

Do you still want to fly an SR–71? OK, let us assume your name is Captain Chuck McGovern, you have spent a long time ferrying H-bombs around the sky in B–52s, and feel you would like a change. Hopefully, you fill in an Air Force Form 215, and send it to SAC headquarters. There your OER, crew professional and medical files will be vetted carefully, and if you pass this hurdle you will be invited to attend the School of Aerospace Medicine at Brooks Air Force Base, San Antonio, Texas.

Known as the Aerospace Research Test Pilot Physical, this is the medical that was devised originally to sort out trainee astronauts. It can take up to ten days, with equal attention to mind and body. Suffice it to say that Col Kardong describes it as probably the most shattering experience he has ever survived personally.

As he leaves Brooks AFB, Chuck McGovern would not quarrel with that assessment. He now knows he is fit enough to fly a Blackbird; but he is still a long way from its cockpit. The results of the medical are assessed by a special board. Their findings then go to the Commander of the 9th Wing at Beale, together with a complete outline of Chuck's career. Reasonably impressed, the Commander invites the would-be SR pilot for a personal interview.

Feeling like a new boy at school, despite the 2,624 hours in his log-book, Chuck is almost surprised to learn at last that he looks good enough to join the élite—which means *really* going back to school.

The USAF discovered long ago that its little T–38 Talon supersonic trainer flies surprisingly like an SR–71. Its approach speed is similar, and vast sums of money can be saved by practising instrument flying on a T–38 instead of in an SR–71. Additional experience in the trainer is not wasted in the slightest, as a T–38 is always kept airborne or at ground alert when a

Blackbird is flying, to assist the SR pilot if he should encounter any in-flight emergency.

Chuck enjoys his time in the T–38. It brings back something of the fun and excitement of the days before he went on to the 'big stuff', and before those grim months in Vietnam. Less attractive are the 135 hours of ground school, and the dozen two-to-four-hour stints in the ground simulator that offers all the toil, sweat and tears of flying, with none of the delights.

Half-way through the simulator course comes the moment about which Chuck has dreamed—now, it seems, so long ago. With one of the Wing's most experienced pilots, he walks across the concrete at Beale towards the aircraft in which he will make his first SR–71 flight. It's not one of the operational 'As' but an SR–71C, looking slightly ungainly with a second pilot's cockpit behind and above the standard one, to give the instructor a good view forward over the head of the pupil. "Some pupil" muses Chuck, thinking of his well-thumbed log-book: but the thought soon passes. Even the non-operational SR–71C is clearly quite an aeroplane, and very different from anything he has flown before.

As he clambers into its cockpit, it seems enormous. In fact, it is far smaller than the B–52 he once flew, but *this* is only a two-seater, a recon-naissance aeroplane, not a vehicle for many tons of bombs and missiles. The SR–71 is virtually a flying fuel tank, with plenty of space inside the 'chines' along each side of the fuselage for the cameras, electronic sensors and other gadgetry of the 'A' model.

Strangely, the cockpit layout is almost an anti-climax. Everything is beautifully positioned (Chuck remembers hearing the Blackbird described many times as a real 'pilot's' aeroplane), but all the buttons, switches and handles look so conventional. Almost the only stranger is an indicator which gives a digital read-out of Mach number, altitude and equivalent airspeed in knots—a reminder that the immense temperatures built up by kinetic heating of the airframe at Mach 3, and the compression of the airflow, makes the standard pressure instruments of little use.

After dual flights with the instructor in the SR–71C, and a check flight, Chuck is ready to team up with his RSO and take his place for the first time in a real SR–71A. Five flights later, they are passed out as a qualified 'mission ready' crew.

Chuck has learned how stable the Blackbird feels, even when flying through turbulence. He has practised formating on a big KC–135 tanker, so that his fuel tanks can be topped up in flight. He has learned to trust the autopilot that flies the aircraft most of the time, just as his RSO has learned the capability of the astro-inertial navigation system that provides automatic star tracking even in daylight. With the entire mission pro-grammed into the aircraft's computer, the RSO need not waste time on navigation and can concentrate on tactical tasks such as communications and fuel management, organising the rendezvous with the KC–135 and operating the complex, highly-secret reconnaissance sensors.

With so much automation, Chuck and his RSO might be considered superfluous; but to 'plug' their brains and hands into the 71's controls and gadgetry demands an immense preparatory operation before take-off.

It all starts the day before the flight is scheduled, when they study a 35mm colour film which outlines all major incidents of the forthcoming mission, including route, refuelling points and target data. In the air, the same film will pass through moving map displays in both cockpits, and will be familiar in every detail.

On the morning of the mission, despite that still-unforgettable medical at Brooks AFB, no crew is cleared for flight without a thorough check by the flight surgeon—and there will be a repeat after landing! Then comes a breakfast of steak and eggs—what the dieticians call a special high-protein low-residue pre-flight meal—eaten to the accompaniment of a briefing by the crew chief on the current status of Chuck's SR–71 and its history of past malfunctions.

The time has come to don the garb of the world's best-dressed recce pilots. It takes up to ten minutes. First long-sleeved, long-legged white underwear with turtleneck, white socks and gloves; then an inner suit of rubber, with several layers of nylon, connected to gloves and boots, so that the whole body is encased in a bladder that can be pressurised to keep the wearer alive at heights where no man was designed to survive.

Next comes the outer suit of aluminium-coated high-temperature nylon, with built-in parachute harness and water-wings. Despite its weight of around 40lb (18kg) the suit is surprisingly comfortable. Even the 'goldfish-bowl' helmet is less claustrophobic than it looks, with its port through which the wearer can drink from a plastic bottle or eat spaceman-like from a tube. This is one part of the operation of which Chuck does not altogether approve. The food tastes reasonable but looks horrible and, like many other Blackbird crew-members, Chuck admits that he would have to be pretty hungry before he would bother to eat it.

With his outfit completed by white boots, fitted with spurs which would hold his legs tightly against the ejection seat if he had to bale out, Chuck is ready to go—almost! In fact, take-off is still about three-quarters of an hour away, as the ground crews must now do all the jobs that make the SR–71 as mission-ready as the men who will occupy its cockpits.

At last, the aircraft is at the end of the long runway. Chuck moves forward the throttles, releases the brakes, sweeps his eyes rapidly over the vital instruments to check that all is well, and selects partial reheat. If the afterburners were switched in fully at this stage, the tyres might be scrubbed off the wheels; so the 71 is already streaking down the runway at a fair speed when a thump in the back confirms full reheat. Chuck eases the long nose up about ten degrees. Effortlessly the big delta begins its climb, already flying faster than the Spitfire and Hurricane fighters which won the Battle of Britain just before Chuck was born.

As they pass 50,000ft (15,250m), he glances through a tiny periscope built into the canopy to check that the toed-in tail-fins are trimmed to zero. In the rear cockpit, the RSO reports to base "Aspen 23 above FL 600"

—flight level 60,000ft (18,300m). Still the 71 goes up, far beyond the heights where there is sufficient water vapour and weather to betray its path with contrails. With the digital Mach reading already looking un-believable, Chuck retracts the navigation lights which might be burned off were they left exposed to the already blistering heat.

"Passing FL700. Start turn in 60 miles (96km), about two minutes." As the Blackbird reaches the pre-planned cruising height and speed, Chuck eases back the throttles and switches to the autopilot which will make that turn far more precisely than a mere human. Already parts of the airframe are heated to more than 1,000 degrees Fahrenheit. What was that Marilyn Monroe film of years back . . . *Some Like it Hot?* Some do, indeed. This is the kind of flying that happens only in dreams—smooth, quiet, comfortable, with 'George' at the controls. Yet there is never a fraction of a second when Chuck is unprepared for a sudden emergency like an inlet restart. Gentle and dreamlike though it may be, the 71 can be completely unforgiving if the crew relax. The pilot must always be conscious of the fact that a one-degree pitch change will push the 71 into a 3,000ft (915m) per minute climb or dive, and the RSO must keep tabs on many things during a 'local flight' that entails a complete circuit of the United States. As they say at Beale: "You've never been lost till you're lost at Mach 3".

While the Blackbird races round the sky at more than 2,000mph (3,200km/h), another 'bird', in Germany, is prepared for a lifetime of reconnaissance, although it goes nowhere—at least while its cameras and electronic sensors are operating.

This is the Kiebitz, or Peewit, built by Dornier at Friedrichshafen, where the big Zeppelins of the German Navy were put together two World Wars ago. It is a strange little craft, with all its 'works' packed inside a conical body, about 4ft (1.20m) in diameter at the bottom and surmounted by a two-blade helicopter rotor.

Kiebitz goes into action packed aboard a truck or tank-like tracked vehicle. In a combat area, it would simply be sent up at the end of a cable, like a robot rotating-wing counterpart of the kite-balloons of 1914–18. With no huge hydrogen-filled gasbag to attract the incendiary fire of enemy fighters, and no inexpendable human observer, it is a true reconnaissance device of the 'seventies, for keeping watch 'over the hill' from a height of 1,000ft (300m) in all weather conditions. Its engine is packed inside the conical body, turning the rotor by simply blowing air through blade-tip nozzles, in the way that a garden sprinkler is spun by water pressure. It can stay up for as long as fuel is pumped through the tether that keeps it from straying.

Over now to a secret USAF air base which might be almost anywhere in the world that can be classed as a potential trouble-spot. On the parking apron are two big Lockheed Hercules turboprop transports. In most respects they differ little from more than a thousand other Hercules' serving with air forces and cargo carriers in every continent; but their nose radome is of a different shape, there are other less familiar excrescences, and the underwing pylons carry what look like miniature aeroplanes rather than the usual long-range fuel tanks.

In fact, these aeroplanes are not always so miniature. One of them, Ryan's Model 154 Firefly, spans 49ft (15m), which is bigger than most fighters.

The story of these 'drones' began back in the mid-thirties, when a famous Hollywood film star had a bright idea. Over in Europe, the RAF and Royal Navy were using radio-controlled, pilotless Tiger Moths for target practice. Although anti-aircraft gunners were usually such poor shots that the aircraft came to no harm, it seemed an awful waste of good aeroplanes. Would not a miniature 'plane, not much bigger than some of the models flown by youngsters, offer just as good a target if it were flown fairly low, at a good speed, under radio control?

So was born the Radioplane company, which was absorbed eventually by one of America's major aerospace concerns, Northrop. It still produces drones for target practice, with deliveries well past the 75,000 mark by the start of this decade; but the worldwide demand for targets has become so great in an age of radar-controlled anti-aircraft guns and missiles that it no longer has the field to itself.

Beech and Ryan have both found the design and manufacture of drones to be big business, and Ryan is even producing a supersonic version of its jet-powered Firebee.

Most of the news stories about such drones concern gunnery and missile-firing practice by troops and fighter pilots. There was, for example, the time when a US pilot dived at supersonic speed on to a Firebee, forgot that cannon shells did not travel nearly as fast as his fighter, caught up the shells he had fired and, literally, shot himself down . . . but this is digressing.

Back in 1965, some strange stories began to appear in the better-informed, or more inquisitive, aviation magazines. The Chinese, it appeared, were claiming that America carried out regular 'spy-flights' over their country, using pilotless aircraft launched from Vietnam. To prove their point, they exhibited at the Chinese People's Revolutionary Museum in Peking the remains of such drones that had been intercepted during their lawless missions.

It was easy to recognise the drones as long-span variants of the Firebee, and gradually the pieces of the jig-saw began to fall into place. The purpose of DC–130 Hercules drone-launching director aircraft at operational bases in countries on the borders of places like China could now be guessed. When a drone much larger than a Firebee made a forced landing on a road-way at Los Alamos, New Mexico, and was photographed by a news agency before it could be removed, the press began to probe into the purpose of what proved to be an early Firefly.

It transpired that several hundred million dollars had been invested in such devices since 1966. Very different from the overgrown models of the 'thirties, Firefly is carefully designed to produce a minimum 'signature' on enemy radar screens. Its turbojet engine is mounted so that it exhausts above the fuselage, offering little 'visible' heat to attract infra-red homing missiles launched from below. Guidance is completely self-contained, with a Doppler radar sensor, inertial navigation system and digital computer, and a command guidance system for final recovery.

Some of the equipment carried by Firefly and other modern USAF drones must remain secret, but the basic reconnaissance sensor is known to be an Itek KA–80A optical bar panoramic camera, with a focal length of 24in (61cm). As the drone wings its way over a target area that could never be overflown by a manned aircraft, this 325lb (147kg) camera can take 1,500 superbly-detailed photographs, each 45in (114cm) long by 4.5in (11.4cm) wide.

Already, Ryan has produced dozens of permutations of its Firebee/ Firefly 'family' of drones, for specialised purposes and with diverse equipment. The Type 147A was little more than a modified Firebee, developed in 90 days in 1962 for the USAF Logistic Command's Big Safari intelligence gathering project. Having proved repeatedly that it could penetrate America's highly-sophisticated defence system undetected, it went into production in various forms, such as the Type 147TE for the Compass Dawn and Compass Dwell programmes (formerly Comfy Bee and Comfy Coat), aimed at the precise pinpointing of enemy ground radars.

Ryan have been permitted to release pictures of many of their drones. One drawing shows no fewer than 20 different types, of which only a handful can be identified positively, and these are by no means all the variants in service or under development. Indeed, others are shown in photographs in this book.

From these photographs, and reconnaissance pictures issued by the Department of Defense, it is possible to build up a picture of a typical operational sortie.

It begins at dusk, when a big DC–130 Hercules lifts into the air from an air base in South Vietnam, carrying under its starboard wing a Ryan 147 drone. More correctly the 147 is known now as an RPV (remotely piloted vehicle) and this is a term that will become increasingly familiar in the years ahead. Many experts will go so far as to suggest that we are on the threshold of the RPV era, in which these pilotless aircraft will take over a high proportion of the tasks currently performed by piloted combat aeroplanes.

This particular DC–130 heads north, but will stay clear of the airspace in which it might be detected by enemy radar and attacked by fighters or surface-to-air missiles. From its nose protrude radomes which form part of the system by which it will direct and control the flight of the 147 through enemy skies.

Time to ignite the turbojet engine of the RPV. A quick check that its systems are operating correctly, and the trapeze structure carrying the 147 is opened to let the little 'spy-plane' begin its night's work. At high sub-sonic speed, its ECM equipment confusing the enemy radars that grope for it vainly, it records an endless tally of information on the locations of the radars, of the surface-to-air missile sites and anti-aircraft gun positions that they control, and a variety of other data that will help the South Vietnamese and their US advisers to know better what is happening on the other side of the demilitarised zone.

Its work done, the 147 heads for home. Meanwhile, a Sikorsky HH–3E 'Jolly Green Giant' helicopter of the USAF Aerospace Rescue and Recovery Service has taken off from a forward base and begins flying towards the spot in the sky where it will rendezvous with the drone. When its electronics indicate that the 147 is near, it transmits a signal which stops the 147's engine and causes its recovery parachute to open. Then, trailing a specially-designed retrieval system, the HH–3E intercepts the rigging lines of the drone's parachute and heads back for base with the 147 suspended below, its 'chute now acting as a drogue to steady it.

Not all such operations are flown by night. The RPVs are fast enough, and well enough protected by ECM equipment, to penetrate even sophisti-cated defences in daylight. Two typical photographs brought back from such sorties show, respectively, a North Vietnamese anti-aircraft gun-site comprising eight camouflaged guns and a gun-laying radar, and a power-line pylon supporting cables under which the drone flew quite safely under control from its DC–130 launch aircraft.

Reconnaissance missions of this kind represent but one way in which RPVs will take over some of the more hazardous combat tasks that now require men to risk their lives. Ryan drones have already been used to drop bombs and launch missiles in demonstrations of their tactical combat potential. In a simulated dogfight with a US Navy Phantom, flown by a highly-skilled crew, an RPV based on the Firebee eluded all the Sparrow and Sidewinder missiles launched at it from the fighter and might itself have destroyed its $2.5 million, Mach 2.5 opponent, and the two men inside, had it been armed to hit back.

The next stage—perhaps already passed by the time these pages are printed—will be to equip those robot 'spy-planes' to seek out targets in enemy territory, attack them with homing missiles and send back to base TV pictures of the operation as it progresses. It will be small consolation for the grounded combat pilot by the control console that he remains in nominal command, simply because his few pounds of grey matter are cheaper, more readily available and less liable to malfunction than elec-tronic circuitry. How far it will be from the kind of flying about which the early pioneers dreamed.

# 12 Reconnais-
# sance in the
# 'Seventies

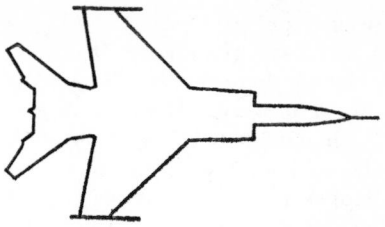

Edging the Atlantic Ocean, half-way down Florida's coastline, lies a triangle of desert wasteland known as Canaveral. Not so many years ago it was inhabited only by the less attractive forms of animal life: snakes, scorpions, horned lizards and armadillos. So prolific were these denizens that Canaveral earned the sobriquet of Florida's Noah's Ark. Its visitors were limited then to those men who earned a living by supplying strange fauna to zoos and private collectors. In 1950 a different kind of man came to Canaveral, the advance guard of the new space age, and in course of time Cape Canaveral was re-named Cape Kennedy, a tribute to the memory of the American President John F. Kennedy.

At the first flush of dawn on April 1st 1960, when the majority of America's citizens were still abed, one area of Canaveral's desolate scrubland was already a hive of activity. Indeed, this had begun days earlier, continuing throughout the nights in the all-revealing glare of arc-lights. On the last day of March the activity had begun to reach a crescendo.

It centred upon the slim shape of a rocket known as Thor-Able, standing erect on its launch ramp. At first it had been almost concealed by the massive steel-girder servicing tower that simplified the task of preparing the rocket for launch. Now, with the moment of flight little more than an hour ahead, the many gantries of the servicing tower had been retracted one by one, and the tower itself withdrawn.

The rocket then stood with only a tall latticework pylon alongside, from which 'umbilical cords' of power cables still fed vital on-board equipment. The moment had come for fuelling, and the more-innocuous kerosene was pumped in first. Then came the liquid oxygen under pressure, and pipework creaked and groaned as the freezing liquid streamed into the rocket's tanks. Soon a coating of frost shrouded pipes and the lower casing of the rocket. The gold and scarlet hues of dawn added highlights to an already colourful scene as, fuelling completed, the preparation crew were withdrawn from the launching ramp.

At this point activity shifted to a concrete blockhouse some 700ft (213m) distant, where the launch team and its director continued the seemingly endless stages of the countdown. Two minutes from launch time external electrical power was cut off, and the rocket's circuits were then maintained by internal batteries. A final check, and with all warning lights indicating a 'go' state, the director thumbed the firing button.

From there on the firing sequence was automatic. At T (launch time) minus 35 seconds ignition began: with 15 seconds to go a deluge of water —some 30,000 US gallons (114,000 litres) per second—streamed below the rocket to cool the flame deflector. At T-minus 10 things began to happen fast: the 'umbilical cords' were detached and fell clear; the vernier motors at the sides of the rocket showed tongues of flame; then, with a mighty roar, the main engines began to belch fire and smoke.

The vibration of power shook loose the coating of ice that had encased the rocket which, restrained by massive steel clamps, was still held firmly to the launch ramp. Only when the engines developed maximum thrust were the clamps released. Slowly at first, balanced on a shimmering cone of flame, the rocket climbed into the elements for which it had been created, the thunder of its engines penetrating the fastness of the block-house, adding its voice to the cheers of the launch team.

Within minutes Thor-Able's payload, a meteorological satellite known as Tiros 1, was placed in an elliptical orbit around the Earth. At its nearest point (perigee) it was 431 miles (694km) above the Earth's surface, at its farthest (apogee) some 471 miles (758km) distant.

As early as 1947 scientists had suggested that a satellite able to photograph cloud systems from high altitude would be a valuable tool for meteorologists; in May 1958 studies were initiated by the American Defense Department's Advanced Research Projects Agency. In October of the same year the project was taken over by NASA, leading to the launch in April 1960.

Tiros, a name derived from Television and Infra-Red Observation Satellite, carried two television cameras powered by nickel-cadmium batteries. Some 9,000 solar cells covered the top and sides of the 290lb (131kg) satellite to re-charge the batteries. Each of the cameras comprised a Vidicon television tube and a focal plane shutter, so arranged that pictures could be 'stored' on the tube's screen. An electron beam converted the 'stored' image into an electronic signal that was then either transmitted direct to ground receivers—if within range—or recorded on magnetic tape. In the latter event, when the satellite was within range of a ground station it could be commanded to relay the data on the tape.

We may never know whether Tiros 1, and more advanced models of the same series that followed it into Earth orbit at a later date, were primarily meteorological or early reconnaissance satellites. Nevertheless, some two hours after launch Tiros 1 was returning to Earth its first television photographs. It was reported that US space scientists expressed themselves as being shocked by highly detailed photographs of the Soviet Union and Communist China taken by the satellite's camera: so detailed that aircraft runways and missile sites could be identified easily.

Whatever the facts, Tiros 1 was, in essence, America's first reconnaissance satellite. Some seven and a half weeks later, on May 24th 1960, the first satellite designated officially as a reconnaissance vehicle was placed successfully into orbit. This was Midas (Missile Defense Alarm System) and subsequent launchings of this and similar vehicles ensured that a continuous watch was maintained on Soviet missile bases.

'Watch' is, perhaps an unsuitable word to describe activities that were not simply of a photographic nature. Midas, for example, relied upon highly-sophisticated infra-red sensors to pinpoint ballistic missile launchings on a worldwide basis. Samos (Satellite and Missile Observation System), the first of which was orbited successfully on January 31st 1961, introduced important new ideas.

Early experience had shown that it was undesirable to place too much reliance on the transmission by conventional radio communications of data stored on magnetic tape. This was due primarily to the fact that the incoming signal frequently suffered deformation from astronomic or atmospheric causes, resulting in loss of detail. It was feared also that an enemy might be able to prevent reception of the intelligence data by 'jamming' or otherwise interfering with the radio signal.

Samos introduced a system of aerial reconnaissance based upon conventional photographic equipment, thus ensuring the resolution of fine detail. This included a capsule especially developed and produced by General Electric, complete with a parachute and a guidance and recovery system. The procedure is for intelligence data to be transmitted back to Earth by radio communications; then, when the satellite is in an appropriate position, the capsule containing the reconnaissance film and other data is ejected and recovered at low level by specially-equipped aircraft.

This 'snatch' recovery technique had first been used to recover the capsules of Discoverer satellites. Specially-equipped Fairchild JC–119 Flying Boxcar aircraft were used successfully for the first time on August 18th 1960, when Discoverer 14 became the first satellite to be recovered in the air. By the time that the USAF's 6593rd Test Squadron, based at Hickam AFB, Hawaii, were required to begin recovery of Samos capsules, they had developed their technique to a stage where they could almost guarantee that 75 per cent of the operations would be successful.

Samos, which was introduced as a reconnaissance satellite in 1961, would appear to continue in service at the time of writing. Details of launchings subsequent to Samos 2 are classified, but it was reported that a satellite of this type was launched on July 22nd 1970, its orbit being such that it could survey areas of the Middle East subject to the Arab-Israeli cease-fire agreement.

In the East the Soviet Union has pursued a similar course, although initially its scientists were a little behind the Americans in orbiting a true reconnaissance satellite. Cosmos 4, launched from their Tyuratam cosmodrome on April 26th 1962, would appear to have been the first successful example, and reports suggest that four more similar launchings were made during 1962. In subsequent years the number of Cosmos launches has increased steadily, and in 1969 rather more than half were made from a new cosmodrome at Plesetsk which became operational in March 1966.

As might be expected, the capability of the Cosmos satellites has increased with the passing of time, and their development has followed a similar pattern to that of their American counterparts. The Russians, however, have applied the name Cosmos to a range of satellites with widely differing capabilities, of which only a proportion have a reconnaissance role.

Cosmos reconnaissance satellites of later vintage were reported to eject capsules for recovery on Earth, a French source suggesting that this activity took place in an area to the north-east of the Aral Sea. It was then assumed that the capsule was landed by parachute, in a similar manner to those of Soviet manned space flights. More recent intelligence leaves little doubt that the French report was a reasoned conclusion based on the possession of certain facts and that, in reality, the Russians have taken a leaf from America's book and are now using the 'snatch' technique to recover the capsules of their reconnaissance satellites.

This makes sense, for considerable time can be saved in gaining vital information if the capsule is recovered in the air. One that is parachuted to Earth need not necessarily touch down in an area of easy access, and valuable time could be lost if the landing was made in the middle of a large lake or on an inaccessible mountain peak.

First intimation that the Soviet Union was adopting this technique came when it was learned that a new type of Cosmos reconnaissance satellite was in use. Analysis of data indicated that the new spacecraft separated into two parts shortly before re-entry, one section being returned for recovery, the other experiencing natural decay and destruction five to ten days later.

The only logical assumption was that the new design had been introduced to reduce the weight or size of the re-entry payload to permit mid-air recovery. The first known use of this satellite came on March 29th 1968, when Cosmos 208 separated into two parts, one of which was recovered on April 2nd. Of a total of 28 recoverable Cosmos launched in 1968, four were of this new type. In 1969 three of 33 were of the new type, and in 1970 eight out of 29. In the first nine months of 1971 no fewer than 12 out of 16 were of the separating type; from this it would appear that the Russians have now developed their 'snatch' technique to a point where it is more effective or economical to deploy an increasing proportion of the separating type.

It is not easy to understand this volte-face in recovery technique on the part of the Russians. It is possible that an unacceptable percentage of Earth-landed capsules have been damaged or difficult to recover: another school of thought has assumed that 'heavy' parachute landings have irreparably damaged the costly reconnaissance camera and that this new technique is aimed at recovering both film and camera. This is pure speculation, only time will reveal the true reasons for the change of heart.

Since both East and West are now involved in the 'snatch' technique, it is worth devoting a few lines to explain how the USAF set about collecting their Samos capsules. With only detail changes, it is the system currently in use for the retrieval of encapsulated information ejected from far more sophisticated satellites.

Due to the vast areas covered by air and space operations of this nature, it was necessary to utilise a long-range long-endurance search and rescue aircraft, and the USAF selected the Lockheed C–130 Hercules for this important role. Two versions resulted: the HC–130H equipped with a nose-mounted recovery system for objects weighing up to 500lb (227kg), and the HC–130N with an air-to-air retrieval system developed by the All American Engineering Company. This latter system has the capability of recovering parachute-suspended packages descending at a rate of 25ft (7.6m)/second, or less, weighing between 65 and 2,500lb (29 and 1,134kg), under daylight VFR conditions at flight altitudes between sea level and 15,000ft (4,570m).

Well-chosen for the task, the Hercules can offer a radius of operation of 1,150 miles (1,850km) and a search at optimum altitude for a period of more than ten hours. The special equipment carried in its capacious fuselage consists of a motor-operated davit and carriage assembly, a retrieval winch, shroud cutter, two hydraulically-operated pole holders with 35ft (10.7m) poles, two air deflectors, a hook and loop assembly, and a control pedestal.

In use, the aircraft's aft cargo door is opened fully and the cargo ramp lowered to a horizontal position; the davit is lowered and the poles carrying the hook and loop assembly are installed in the holders and fully extended to the rear of the aircraft. Slack is taken in on the retrieval winch, and an automatic brake is set to correspond with the weight of the load to be recovered. All is now ready and the Hercules orbits the predicted re-entry area.

Although the recovery exercise itself is basically simple, the overall success of the mission requires that the Hercules should be in exactly the right place at the right time. The determination of this factor is not easy, for an error of a fraction of a second in firing the retro-rockets of the re-entry vehicle can alter the calculated impact point by many miles.

Visual sighting of the capsule and its parachute would be far too hit-and-miss; so the Hercules carries a tracker system that locks-on to a beacon signal transmitted from the capsule as it enters the atmosphere. This signal, converted by the tracker system, gives the pilot and navigator a heading and attitude reference displayed on needle indicators. Should the system lose its lock on the beacon, a memory subsystem extrapolates a plot for 15 seconds, based on previous readings. If at the end of this period the signal has not been re-located, the system reverts automatically to the search role.

For the crew of the Hercules their countless hours of training culminate in a moment of great excitement as the tracker signals a bearing. Quickly but calmly, the huge aircraft is turned on to the indicated heading and, throttles well forward, the note of the four 4,500hp turboprop engines rises in seemingly-matching excitement as they thrust the Hercules towards its mid-air rendezvous.

Restless eyes quarter the vast panorama of sky, every crewman anxious to be first to spot the blossoming parachute and its vital cargo. This time the navigator wins the lottery: there it is, dead ahead, but well above their altitude. The engines are given maximum power as the pilot eases the control column back to attain the best possible rate of climb. Height is essential, for if the first attempt fails there may still be time for a second pass at lower level.

This is a moment for the exercise of real piloting skill, manoeuvring the aircraft so that the hook and loop assembly, trailing behind the extended poles, snares the parachute falling towards the sea. A slight bank, stick forward to drop the aircraft's nose and 'contact'. The winch line screams out as if a giant fish has been hooked, until stopped smoothly by the automatic brake as the 'catch' is accelerated to the forward speed of the aircraft. The rest is routine, and the capsule is soon winched in and safely tied-down within the Hercules. Operation successful!

Thus we have arrived at a situation where the two great and opposing military powers have the means to keep themselves aware of developments in the opposing camp. This is fine: it is what President Eisenhower's Open Skies policy was all about, but it needed also mutual agreement for arms limitation.

Until signature of the SALT agreement, following $2\frac{1}{2}$ years of Strategic Arms Limitation Talks between America and Russia, in May 1972, we had only the reconnaissance aspect of Open Skies. Whilst this made it possible to maintain an effective policy, each nation being able to learn with little delay of military developments on the other side, it led to continually rising expenditure on the means of maintaining the deterrent.

At the beginning of November 1967, for example, Mr McNamara, then US Secretary of Defense, announced that the Soviet Union appeared to be developing a 'space bomb'. This was described as a Fractional Orbital Bombardment System (FOBS) that could be launched into orbit some 100 miles (160km) above the Earth's surface. At a given point, before completion of the first orbit, the weapon could be slowed by the firing of retro-rockets, so causing it to fall on a predetermined target. Though expected to be less accurate and more costly than conventional ICBMs, it offered the advantages—so far as the Russians were concerned—of striking with far less warning and of making its attack from the south, a direction completely in opposition to that for which American early-warning radar systems had been established.

Not only was it desirable that the US should itself develop a similar deterrent weapon, it was essential to remain constantly aware of the status of the FOBS programme. Reconnaissance was the answer, and on November 6th 1970, a first attempt was made to launch a new reconnaissance satellite, known as an Integrated Missile Early Warning Satellite (IMEWS).

This first attempt was rated as unsuccessful since the satellite failed to enter the desired orbit, which is believed to be a synchronous one with an inclination of approximately 10°. This would make the spacecraft trace out a figure-eight ground track at a fixed longitude such that, when it was north of the Equator, its sensors and camera would gain a better view of northern Russia.

Data provided by Britain's Royal Aircraft Establishment in mid-1971 suggested that the first IMEWS was far from being a complete failure, as it had been possible to correct the initial highly eccentric orbit to one with a perigee of 16,200 miles (26,170km) and apogee of 22,400 miles (36,050km) at an inclination of 8°, resulting in a longitudinal drift. The spacecraft's equipment was in no way affected by this orbital error, and it is reported that the USAF was able to test and prove the efficiency of this equipment, by monitoring many of America's own space launches. In this manner, it was possible to gain valuable information on the early-warning capability of the system.

A second attempt, on May 5th 1971, put an IMEWS in geostationary orbit (ie, remaining at a constant spot above the Earth's surface) over the Indian or Pacific Ocean. This, and similar satellites, are able to maintain a constant watch for long-range missile firings by either Communist China or the Soviet Union.

The satellites 'watch' in more ways than one: by detecting heat emission from enemy missiles by means of an infra-red sensor, believed to employ a 2,000-element detector operating in the 3–5 micron region, and by a visible light sensor (VLS)—a TV camera type of device—which is thought to enable military observers to see the rocket plume of ICBMs as they are launched and rise above the atmosphere. It is possible that IMEWS may also carry Vela-type sensors, able to detect X-ray, gamma-ray and neutron emissions.

The two main types of sensor are used to complement each other and prevent false warnings. If the infra-red sensors detect an ICBM launch, it is believed that the satellite then transmits a VLS signal to permit evaluation of the infra-red alarm. In the absence of infra-red warnings, VLS signals are transmitted at periodic intervals to confirm that the infra-red detectors are operative and that they have not missed 'seeing' an ICBM launch.

Data gained by the IMEWS satellites is transmitted first to two ground stations, one located in Guam and the other some 300 miles (483km) north of Adelaide, Australia, believed to be at Narrungar in Woomera. The information is then relayed, via a communications satellite, to NORAD (North American Air Defense Command) headquarters at Colorado Springs, Colorado.

Intelligence gained by satellites of this kind, supplementing special reconnaissance aircraft, has already confirmed the existence of a Soviet MRV (multiple re-entry vehicle). This is a type of warhead that deploys three separate re-entry vehicles, and obviously these present a far more difficult interception problem than that posed by a single warhead. More importantly, study of photographs provided by aircraft and satellites has shown that the separate warheads re-enter the atmosphere to impact in a pattern which is similar to the 'footprint' of three Minuteman ICBMs dispersed in their underground silos.

America was already ahead of this move, for in 1965 the proposed development of a new Fleet Ballistic Missile Weapon System (FBMWS) had been announced. Named Poseidon C3, this was to be a two-stage missile for underwater or surface launching, and was intended to replace the Polaris missiles of the USN's missile submarines. It was a step ahead of the Soviet MRV concept, for it was proposed that it should have Multiple Independently-targetable Re-entry Vehicles (MIRV), and development flight testing of 20 of these missiles had been completed by June 19th 1970.

The concept of using submarines to deploy nuclear weapons had, at one time, seemed to offer an ultimate weapon that would be sufficient to deter any adversary from making a nuclear attack. This was based upon the assumption that a nuclear-powered submarine, operating at an unknown position within the oceans that cover seven-tenths of the Earth's surface, would be virtually impossible to detect.

Today, the emphasis of US aerospace reconnaissance technology is on methods that will accurately pinpoint the position of enemy submarines. Much has already been done, and the development of aircraft such as the Lockheed S–3A Viking carrier-based anti-submarine aircraft, mentioned in an earlier chapter, represents but a first step in this direction.

Infra-red devices, when fully developed, should have the capability of detecting nuclear submarines at considerable depth. This is due to the fact that such vessels, with nuclear power plants, use large amounts of sea water to cool the nuclear reactors. As the cooling water does its job its temperature is increased, and it has been reported that advanced sensors used on some reconnaissance satellites have the capability of detecting the slightly increased temperature in a submarine's wake at unspecified but considerable depths.

Other techniques have been or are being developed that have great future significance for reconnaissance activities. Techniques that seem to offer development scope for anti-submarine detection emanate from more conventional photographic sources. Ironically, one that shows great promise was first evolved in Russia, where it was given the name of Spectra-zonal photography. Known more commonly as the 'false-colour' technique, it relies upon the use of a special film stock exposed through a yellow filter. When developed it produces yellowish pictures of dry surfaces, while damp areas are shown in varying degrees of cyan blue, increasing in intensity over water and becoming darker as the depth increases. This has proved valuable in reconnaissance pictures of coastal and delta areas.

Aerial Ektachrome, a colour film stock produced by the Eastman Kodak company, also has interesting potential for oceanic reconnaissance. Used originally for aerial survey purposes, it was soon found that shallow and deep water were recorded by a wide variation of colour, ranging from sandy yellow to intense blue respectively. It needs little imagination to appreciate that the solid bulk of a submarine on patrol can affect locally the visually-recorded water depth and, by inference, the colour record.

A more 'way out' system involves the use of electronic sensors capable of producing apparently featureless prints that appear uniformly grey to the human eye. When a series of pictures is produced by using colour filters of varying wave-lengths to reveal the 'invisible', it is astounding what detail appears in the form of different coloured shapes.

A photograph of the mouth of the Colorado River, brought back by Gemini 4 astronauts, was subjected to this treatment. Taken from a height of some 120 miles (193km) it revealed no unusual detail in its original form. After the specialised treatment, schools of fish and hidden shoals were revealed with surprising clarity. It is not unreasonable to suppose that a device which can 'photograph' a school of fish, perhaps some 200ft (61m) below the surface of the sea, may eventually be developed to a point where it will ensure that there is no hiding place for a nuclear submarine.

Thus the reconnaissance wheel has more-or-less turned full circle. While it does not appear that the Soviet Union yet has in service an early-warning space surveillance system comparable to the USAF's IMEWS, it has been reported that Soviet spacecraft may carry Midas and Vela-type sensors. As in World War I, we have reached a position where surveillance capability is such that it appeared necessary to devise means of destroying the reconnaissance source itself.

First hints of such measures came when intelligence sources reported that certain Soviet spacecraft with Cosmos designations appeared to have the capability of intercepting and destroying other satellites. Early 'interceptors' of this type are believed to have included Cosmos 249, 252, 374 and 375. Cosmos 394 for example, launched on February 9th 1971, appears to have intercepted and destroyed Cosmos 397, that was launched sixteen days later. Similarly, Cosmos 400, launched on March 19th 1971, was subsequently 'intercepted' by Cosmos 404 on April 3rd 1971.

Other reports have indicated that the Soviet Union is attempting to extend this capability to make possible the destruction of satellites orbiting the Earth at low altitude. This represents a far more difficult interception problem, for as the altitude of the target decreases its speed in relation to a fixed ground position is far higher, thus allowing far less reaction time.

This information derives from intelligence reports to the effect that Cosmos 462, launched from Tyuratam on December 3rd 1971, was destroyed subsequently by Cosmos 459 at a height of only 143 miles (230km). This is a far more significant achievement than the destruction of Cosmos 400, which was reportedly at an altitude of some 550 miles (885km) at the moment of interception.

Such a capability posed the question for many months as to why the Soviet Union had made no efforts to destroy the US satellites which are constantly maintaining a close watch on all of its military activities.

The most sensible guess is that Soviet reconnaissance had already ascertained that the Americans have a similar capability, so that the Russians realised that action on their part would initiate similar reaction from the US side. It was far better for them to know, by maintenance of their own reconnaissance activities, the state of development of the American offensive and defensive forces. This applied also in reverse, for a report as recent as March 13th, 1972, suggested the existence of two US anti-satellite defence systems designated by USAF Codes 437 and 922.

The SALT agreement has made reconnaissance satellites 'respectable' by stipulating that they must be permitted to do their job without hindrance, as the primary guarantee of good faith by both sides. Nonetheless, it is likely that the Americans, at least, will equip their future early warning and vital military communications satellites with alarms that will give warning of attack.

Clearly this is important. Non-receipt of data from the defensive reconnaissance network could conceivably be due to a communications system malfunction. It is essential to be able to determine if this is the case or, of more sinister import, whether the source of information itself has been destroyed.

Two complementary devices have been proposed: proximity warning sensors to signal the close approach of another space vehicle, and impact sensors to give warning of a destructive attack. The latter device is likely to be an independent subsystem, several effectively isolated sensors being installed on each satellite to enhance the likelihood that at least one might survive long enough to signal an alert.

It would seem, therefore, that citizens of both East and West must expect to face ever-mounting costs. Parity in deterrence and surveillance is the only means of maintaining a state of 'peace' until such time as a miracle of enlightenment brings a desire for genuine disarmament and an all-time ban on nuclear and thermonuclear weapons. This will remain true so long as the two major military powers advance in destructive capability at a similar rate, and provided a third factor, such as unpredictable intervention by Red China, doesn't upset the *status quo*.

Unfortunately, 'if' is the longest two-letter word in the English language —and one that can upset the best-laid plans.

Hint of such an 'if' came early in 1972 from John S. Foster Jr, director of US defense research and engineering. He indicated that there was evidence to suggest that the Soviet Union was determined at all costs to surpass American technological skills. Furthermore, during the previous twelve months US information-gathering sources had become aware that the Russians had developed new military capabilities. The Department of Defense indicated that the Soviet Union had already achieved technical superiority in anti-ballistic missile systems, fractional orbital bombardment systems, strategic air-defence interceptors, tactical anti-shipping missiles, surface attack ships, anti-aircraft artillery systems, some armoured combat vehicles, medium- and high-altitude surface-to-air missile defences, surface-to-surface tactical missiles and heavy-life helicopters.

Foster had no doubt of the importance to the entire Western world of American retention of overall technological superiority, thus allowing a realistic appreciation of the capability of any potential adversary. 'Once we appear to have lost that capability,' he said, 'we lose our ability to measure our relative strength and to compete effectively, and in due course we should lose confidence in the realism of our deterrence. . . .'

In the pages of this book we have already learnt something of the meaning of an effective deterrent. More importantly, we should have gained some appreciation of the part that aerial and satellite reconnaissance can play in providing the in-depth intelligence needed to maintain the kind of delicate parity established by the SALT agreement, in terms of both strategic offensive missiles and anti-ballistic missile systems.

There is no reason to suppose that leaders in the United States are not fully aware of this grave responsibility; or that they are ignorant of the part which reconnaissance has to play in maintaining a peace that, however costly or uneasy, is infinitely preferable to a war that can only bring worldwide devastation.

On the contrary, there is every indication that the Americans appreciate fully the vital and continuing role of reconnaissance, and this is confirmed by recent reports of new 'spy' satellites which are already operational or in the planning stage.

Among those currently in use are photo-reconnaissance types used for search-and-find missions. These have the job of wide-scale coverage of the Earth's surface, in sufficient detail to allow skilled interpreters to spot anything new or significant. Photographs are taken by a camera that is equipped with a lens of moderate resolution and the film is processed on-board. This film is then scanned by a laser beam device which converts the image into electronic signals that can be transmitted back to Earth via seven receiving stations dotted around the globe.

As we have already seen, pictures transmitted in this way can suffer loss of detail and could be subject to interference from enemy sources. This is not vitally important in relation to a device whose surveillance task is general rather than specific. Immediately an interpreter sees something suspicious, or which he considers worthy of closer investigation, he is able to call upon the services of another new satellite.

This, known as a close-look satellite, is equipped usually with a high-resolution camera, but can also carry multi-spectral cameras. Deployed in an orbit that covers the requisite area, these cameras can supply the detailed coverage required; after some two weeks in orbit, the exposed film—which has been fed into a nose-capsule—is returned to Earth and recovered by the aircraft 'snatch' technique.

The two types of satellites have, working in conjunction, provided important information on Russian silos for the storage and launch of ICBMs. Early in 1971 a search-and-find mission disclosed unusual activity, and subsequent close-look inspection confirmed a number of new silos.

Stepped-up usage of the two satellites was able to confirm, by the end of May 1971, that about 60 of the new Soviet silos had been discovered. It was even possible to differentiate between two types of silos with diameters that varied by about four feet (1.22m).

It soon became apparent, however, that the use of these two types of satellites was both costly and time-consuming. Most important was the latter factor, for evidence uncovered by a search-and-find mission could not receive immediate close-look examination.

This was no new discovery, for in the mid-1960s when a manned orbiting laboratory (MOL) had been planned, one important advantage claimed for the concept was the prospect of astronauts carrying out a search-and-find exercise with suitable telescopes. Any object worthy of close study would then be photographed by high-resolution cameras and the resulting film returned to Earth via a capsule that would be recovered by a 'snatch' aircraft.

Since that time advancing technology has made it possible for the American aerospace industry to develop a satellite which can satisfy these functions automatically. Thus it carries out a continuous search-and-find mission, the processed film being scanned and the electronic photo-image transmitted back to Earth bases.

If an interpreter discovers an object of interest, he can command the satellite to use its high-resolution camera during its next orbit and thus, within a much reduced period of time, it is possible to have available close-look evidence that comes to hand via the 'snatch' aircraft.

This satellite, known unofficially as Big Bird, consists essentially of a modified Lockheed Agena some 50ft (15.2m) in length and 10ft (3.05m) in diameter. It carries an enormous camera that is reported to be capable of such high resolution that even from orbital heights of more than 100 miles (160km) objects as small as 1ft (0.3m) across can be seen and identified. The first of these new-generation satellites was launched on June 15th 1971, a second on January 20th 1972.

It is clear that Big Bird gives the West the capability of faster and more detailed surveillance of the Soviet Union and Red China. Despite the fact that it is the 'latest and greatest', even this advanced concept has its limitations, particularly in respect of the time lapse between the first glimpse of an interesting subject and the moment when close-look photographs are available for detailed inspection.

Advanced plans to bridge this time gap are already on the drawing board. A TRW Systems/USAF project, which is coded 1010, is intended to provide real-time close-look reconnaissance, with on-board equipment to process the film exposed by high-resolution cameras. Instead of ejecting the film by capsule, new-generation scanning systems will convert the image into electronic signals that will be flashed back to Earth via a Data Relay Satellite. A similar project, coded 749, is being developed to provide the USN with real-time oceanic surveillance.

The availability of such equipment, planned for 1976–77, will give the West continuous almost-live surveillance of the territory of any potential enemy. This is the kind of reconnaissance that could bring an Open Skies policy fully to life, for it would be impossible for an aggressor to build, test and deploy an all-powerful strategic weapon without the 'other side' being aware of every detail. Awareness is safety.

US President Lyndon B. Johnson is reported to have said that reconnaissance satellites are the most important single device ever built by the US. He added that if the total money spent by America on space exploration was multiplied tenfold, and the only tangible results had been reconnaissance satellites, then the money would have been well spent.

He certainly knew what he was talking about!

# Index

'A' camera  25
A–1E Skyraider aircraft  82
A–7 Corsair II aircraft  97
A–11 aircraft  102
ABC ('Airborne Cigar')  49
ABM (anti-ballistic missile)  91, 92
ABRES (Advanced Ballistic Re-Entry System)  91
ADC (Air Defense Command) USAF  75
Adsid (Air-Delivered Seismic Detection sensor)  98, 99
AEW (airborne early warning)  97
AI (airborne interception) radar  48
ALE–29B Chaff dispenser  100
ALQ–99 noise jamming system  100
ALQ–100 deception ECM (DECM)  100
An–22 (Antonov 'Cock') aircraft  13
ASW (anti-submarine warfare)  93, 95, 97
AWACS (airborne warning and control system)  97, 101
Abel, Col Rudolf  70
Acoubuoy acoustic sensor  98
Acousid acoustic sensor  98
Adana (Turkey)  67, 68, 73
Advanced Research Projects Agency, US  112
Aerial Ektachrome film  118
Aerial Kodacolor film  58
Aerospace Rescue and Recovery Service (USAF)  110
Aerospace Research Test Pilot Physical  104
Aérostiers, Company of  18
Agena satellite  122
Aisne, Battle of the  24
Albatros aircraft  26
Arvin troops  82
Augenstein, Hauptmann Hans-Heinz  52
Autolycus ionisation detector  93

B–17 Flying Fortress aircraft  50, 51
B–29 Superfortress aircraft  44
B–47 Stratojet aircraft  60
B–52 Stratofortress aircraft  74, 75, 99, 100, 103–105
B–58 Hustler aircraft  103
B.E.2 aircraft  20, 22, 23, 26
Be–12 (Beriev 'Mail') aircraft  92
Bf 109 aircraft  39
'Badger' (Tupolev Tu–16) aircraft  90, 92
Beale AFB, California  102
'Bear' (Tupolev Tu–95) aircraft  89, 90, 92
Beaufighter aircraft  41, 48
Bell HU–1 aircraft  84

Beriev Be–12 'Mail' aircraft  92
Berlin (Germany)  32–35, 50, 54, 55
Big Bird satellite  122
'Big Safari'  109
Bird Dog aircraft  80–82, 96
'Blackbird'  102–107
'Black Crow'  97, 99
Blenheim aircraft  39
Blériot XI monoplane  21
Blériot, Louis  19
'Blinder' (Tupolev Tu–22) aircraft  92
'Blue Charger'  97, 100
Bomber Command, RAF  39–43, 47–49
Bonanza aircraft  99
Braun, Dr Wernher von  43
Britain, Battle of  38, 106
British Expeditionary Force  21, 22, 25
Bronco aircraft  96, 97
Brooks AFB, Texas  104, 106
Bruneval (France)  39, 40, 42

'C' camera  25
C3 Poseidon missile  118
C–47 aircraft  43, 96
C–119 aircraft  96
CIA (Central Intelligence Agency)  66, 68, 73
CRT (cathode-ray tube)  94, 95
Cairo (Egypt)  11, 31, 32
Campbell, Lt C. D. M.  24
Canberra aircraft  87
Cape Kennedy (USA)  111
Caproni 161bis aircraft  65
Castro, Fidel  72
Cathode-ray tube (CRT)  94, 95
'Cefirm Leader'  97
'Cefirm Scavenger'  97
'Chaff'  100
Chain Home radar  39
Charles, Professor  17
Chinese People's Revolutionary Museum  108
Churchill, Winston S.  42
'Circle 10' missions  57
Civil War, American  18
'Cleat' (Tupolev Tu–114) aircraft  101
Coastal Command, RAF  41
'Cobra Ball'  92
'Cock' (Antonov An–22) aircraft  13
Cody, 'Colonel' S. F.  20
Colorado River (USA)  119
Colorado Springs (USA)  117
'Combat Angel'  97
'Comfy Bee'  97, 109
'Comfy Coat'  109
'Commando Bolt'  97, 99

Company of Aérostiers 18
'Compass Cope' 97
'Compass Dawn' 97, 109
'Compass Dwell' 97, 109
'Compass Ghost' 97
'Compass Quick' 97
'Concrete-dibber' bomb 11
Constellation aircraft 90, 98, 99
'Coot' (Ilyushin Il–18) aircraft 92
Corsair II aircraft 97
Corse, 2nd Air Mechanic W.D. 24
Cosmos satellites 113, 114, 119
Cotton, Sidney 28–37, 40
Coutelle, Capt J. M. J. 17, 18
Cox, Flt Sgt C. W. H. 40
'Crosslegs' 97
Crusader aircraft 76, 77

DC–130 Hercules aircraft 108–110
Dakota aircraft 43, 96
'Dambusters' 44
'Dartboard' transmitter 50
Dassault Mirage aircraft 95
Data Relay Satellite 122
de Morveau, Guyton 17
Department of Defense, US 91, 92, 109, 120
Discoverer satellite 113
Dittmar, Heini 43
Domodedovo Airport, Moscow (USSR) 13
Dornberger, Major-General Walter 43
Dornier Do 17 aircraft 46
*Drachen* kite-balloon 18
Draken aircraft 95
Dufaycolor Company 28, 29, 32

E–2 Hawkeye aircraft 101
EA–6B Intruder aircraft 100, 101
EC–121M Constellation aircraft 90
EC–121R Constellation aircraft 98, **99**
EC–135 aircraft 90, 91
ECCM (electronic counter-counter-measures) 97
ECM (electronic countermeasures) 52, 85, 89, 91, 94, 97, 100, 110
Elint (electronic intelligence) 97, 100
ERASE 97
Egyptian Air Force 11
Eisenhower, Dwight D. 59–61, 64, 70, 79, 116
Electra Model 12A aircraft 30
Emil Emil airborne radar 47, 48

F–4 Phantom aircraft 13–15, 95, 97–99, 101, 110
F–14 Tomcat aircraft 100
F24 camera 31
F–86 Sabre aircraft 12, 56
F–100 Super Sabre aircraft 81
F–105D Thunderchief aircraft 96
FAC (Forward Air Controller) 80–83, 99
FAN (Forward Air Navigator) 83

FBMWS (Fleet Ballistic Missile Weapon System) 118
F.E. aircraft 23
FLIR (Forward-looking infra-red) 94
FOBS (Fractional Orbital Bombardment System) 116, 118
FuG 10 HF radio 47
FuG 16 VHF radio 49
FuG 202 *Lichtenstein BC* airborne radar 48
FuG 220 *Lichtenstein SN–2* airborne radar 50
FuG 227 *Flensburg* homing device 50
FuG 350 *Naxos Z* homing device 50
Faroes gap 89, 90
'Ferret' aircraft 47
Fighter Command, RAF 38, 40
Firebee drone 108, 110
Firefly drone 108, 109
Fleet Air Arm 41
Fleurus, Battle of 18
*Flugwachen* listening posts 46
Fokker monoplane 22, 23
Fortress aircraft 50, 51
Foster, John S. Jr 120, 121
'Foxbat' (Mikoyan MiG–23) aircraft 13
Freya radar 39, 45, 46
Fritsch, Colonel-General Baron von 38, 44

GCI (Ground Controlled Interception) 46
Galland, General Adolf 52
'Gee' radio navigation aid 42
Gemini spacecraft 119
German Naval Airship Division 20
German Navy 20, 107
Glenn, John 76
Goering, Reichsmarschall Hermann 32, 34, 38, 46, 49, 51
Grey, Spenser 28
'Ground Grocer' 48, 51
'Guideline' surface-to-air missile 100, 101
Gulf of Suez 14, 15

$H_2S$ airborne radar 42, 50
HC–130H aircraft 114
HC–130N aircraft 114
HH–3E aircraft 110
Hobos (Homing Bomb System) 99
HU–1 aircraft 84
Halifax aircraft 51
Harrier aircraft 95, 96
Harvard aircraft 57
'Have Fault' 97, 99
'Have Lemon' 97
'Have Orchid' 97
Hawker P.1121 aircraft 13
Hawkeye aircraft 101
*Helle Nachtjagd* 46
Hemming, Maj 'Lemnos' 41
Hercules aircraft 107, 108, 115, 116

Heston aerodrome (UK)   36, 40
Hickham AFB, Hawaii   113
'High Fix'   97
Hill, Sqn Ldr Tony   39
*Himmelbett*   46
'Hip Pocket'   97
Hitler, Adolf   29, 34, 43
Ho Chi Minh Trail   98, 99
Hodgson, J. E.   18
Huey aircraft   84
Hurricane aircraft   41, 106
Hustler aircraft   103

ICBM (Intercontinental Ballistic Missile)   69, 91, 92, 116, 117, 122
Il–18 (Ilyushin 'Coot') aircraft   92
Il–38 (Ilyushin 'May') aircraft   92
IMEWS (Integrated Missile Early Warning Satellite)   116, 117, 119
IOIS (Integrated Operational Intelligence System)   85
ISC (Infiltration Surveillance Centre)   98, 99
'Igloo White'   98, 99
Ilyushin Il–18 'Coot' aircraft   92
  Il–38 'May' aircraft   92
Incirlik AFB, Adana (Turkey)   67
Interception Alert Force, RAF   88
Intruder aircraft   97, 100, 101

JC–119 aircraft   113
Johnson C. L. 'Kelly'   61, 64, 65, 71
Johnson, Lyndon B   102, 123
Jones, H. A.   23, 25
'Jostle'   51
Joubert de la Ferté, Capt Philip   20
Jourdan, General   18
Junkers Ju 88 aircraft   46, 48, 50

K–13 missile   14
KA–80A camera   109
KB–18A camera   94
KC–135 aircraft   91, 105
KGB   64
Kammhuber, General   46, 49
Kardong, Lt-Col G. Abe   103
Kennedy, John F.   72, 74, 75, 77, 111
Kiebitz reconnaissance drone   107
Kill Devil Hills, North Carolina (USA)   19
Kite-balloon   18
Korean War   55, 56, 58, 59, 82, 83
Krause, Hauptmann Hans   52
Krushchev, Premier   70, 78

Lancaster aircraft   49
Land camera   66
Langemarck, Battle of   26
Laughlin AFB, Texas (USA)   73
Laws, Flt Sgt F. C. V.   24
League of Nations   54
Leica camera   31, 33, 35
Liberator aircraft   51

*Lichtenstein* airborne radar   48
Lightning aircraft   88–90
Lindemann, Professor   42
Lockheed Aircraft Company   64
Logistics Command, USAF   109
'Long Talk'   97
Los Alamos (New Mexico)   108
Lubyanka prison, Moscow (USSR)   64, 70
*Luftwaffe*   38, 45–52
Lysander aircraft   39

MAD (magnetic anomaly detection)   94
Me 110 aircraft   39, 46, 48, 52
Me 163 aircraft   43
Midas (Missile Defense Alarm System)   113, 119
MiG–15 (Mikoyan 'Fagot') aircraft   12, 15, 56
MiG–17 (Mikoyan 'Fresco') aircraft   12
MiG–19 (Mikoyan 'Farmer') aircraft   12
MiG–21 (Mikoyan 'Fishbed') aircraft   13, 14
MiG–23 (Mikoyan 'Foxbat') aircraft   12–15, 101
MiG aircraft   73, 90, 100
MIRV (Multiple Independently-target-able Re-entry Vehicle)   118
MOL (Manned Orbiting Laboratory)   15, 16, 122
MRV (Multiple Re-entry Vehicle)   91, 117
Mackenzie-Wishart slide   25
'Mandrel'   47, 51
Mannheim (Germany)   30, 34, 47
Mapplebeck, Lt Gilbert   21
Marix, Reggie   28
Marne, Battle of the   22
Maryland aircraft   41
'May' (Ilyushin Il–38) aircraft   92
McCoy AFB, Florida (USA)   77
McNamara, US Secretary of Defense   116
Minuteman ICBM   118
Mirage aircraft   95
Missile Defense Alarm System (Midas)   113, 119
Model 12A Electra aircraft   30
Model 154 Firefly drone   108
Model 337 Super Skymaster aircraft   83
Moehne dam (Germany)   44
Mohawk aircraft   100
'Monica' radar   50
Mons (Belgium)   21, 89
'Moon Cone'   97
Moore-Brabazon, Lt J. T. C.   24
Morveau, Guyton de   17
Moselle, Army of the   18
Mosquito aircraft   41, 45, 50, 51
'Moss' (Tupolev Tu–114) aircraft   92, 101
Munich (Germany)   50
Munich Crisis   28
Munster (Germany)   50

NASA (National Aeronautics and Space Administration) 92, 112
NATO (North American Treaty Organisation) 13, 89, 92
NORAD (North American Air Defense Command) 117
Nagasaki (Japan) 44
Nasser, Colonel 13
National Photographic Interpretation Center 72
Nene turbojet engine, Rolls-Royce 12
Nile, Battle of the 18
Nimrod MR1 aircraft 93
Niven, Bob 30, 31, 33–37
Nixon, President Richard 90
Nuremberg (Germany) 50

O–1 Bird Dog aircraft 82
O–2 aircraft 83, 99
OER (Officers' Evaluation Report) 103, 104
OV–1D Mohawk aircraft 100
OV–10 Bronco aircraft 96, 97
'Oboe' radio navigation aid 42
'One Eye' 97
'Open Skies' policy 60, 61, 66, 79, 116, 123
'Operation Corona' 45, 46, 49

P.3 airship 20
P331 radar 95
P.1121 aircraft 13
PI (Photographic Interpreter) 37, 60, 72, 73, 76, 77
PR (Photo Reconnaissance) units 24, 25, 56
PRU (Photographic Reconnaissance Units) 41
Paine, Commodore Godfrey 28
Parseval, von 19
Pathfinder squadrons, RAF 42, 43
'Pave Eagle' 97, 99
Pawlak, Capt H. J. 82
Peck, Air Vice-Marshal 36, 37
Peenemünde (Germany) 42, 43
'Peewit' reconnaissance drone 107
'People Sniffer' 84
Pezzi, Mario 65
Phantom aircraft 13–15, 87, 95, 97–99, 101, 110
Photographic Development Unit 41
Photographic Interpretation Unit 43
Piazza, Capt 19
'Piperack' 51
Plesetsk (USSR) 114
Polaris missile 118
Polaroid camera 66
Poseidon C3 missile 118
Powers, Francis Gary 64, 70, 71, 103
'Puff Ball' 97

Q–26 aircraft 84
QU–22B aircraft 99

Quail decoy 100
'Quick Fix' 97
'Quick Look' 97, 100

RA–5C Vigilante aircraft 85, 86
RAAF (Royal Australian Air Force) 55
RAE (Royal Aircraft Establishment) 117
RAF (Royal Air Force) 23, 26, 36, 44, 45, 48–51, 89, 95, 108
RB–47 aircraft 60
RB–57F aircraft 87
R.E. aircraft 23
R.E.8 aircraft 26
RF–4C Phantom aircraft 87
RF–8A Crusader aircraft 76, 77
RF–101 Voodoo aircraft 76, 78
RFC (Royal Flying Corps) 20, 21, 23, 24
RN (Royal Navy) 108
RNAS (Royal Naval Air Service) 28
RPV (remotely piloted vehicle) 109, 110
RSO (reconnaissance systems officer) 103, 105–107
RU–21 aircraft 97
Red Top missile 88, 89
Richards, Denis 40
Richthofen, von 26
Royal Aircraft Factory 20, 26
Rudenko, Roman 70
Ryan Firebee drone 108
Model 154 Firefly drone 108

S–3A Viking aircraft 93, 118
SAC (Strategic Air Command) USAF 73, 75, 100, 103, 104
SALT (Strategic Arms Limitation Talks) agreement 116, 120, 121
SAM (Surface-to-air missile) 70, 73, 85
Samos (Satellite and Missile Observation System) 113, 114
SHAPE (Supreme Headquarters of the Allied Powers in Europe) 89
SR–71A aircraft 102, 103, 104, 106, 107
SR–71C aircraft 105
SS–9 missile 92
Saab Draken aircraft 95
Sabre aircraft 12, 56
Sadat, President 11
Saigon (Vietnam) 85
Saldivar, Fulgencio Batista 72
Salisbury Plain (UK) 20
San Cristobal (Cuba) 73, 78
Saturn/Apollo 91
Schillig Roads 35, 39
Schmid, General 45, 49, 51
Schoene, Herr 32
School of Aerospace Medicine (USAF) 104
'See Saw' 97
Senso 94
'Serrate' 48, 50
'Shadow' gunship aircraft 96
'Short Horn' 97

Sidcot suit  28
Sidewinder missile  110
Siegfried Line  30, 33, 34, 41
Sigsfeld, von  19
Sikorsky HH–3E aircraft  110
Six-day War (1967)  11, 15
Sixth Fleet, US  12
'Skip Spin'  97
'Ski-sites'  44
'Skunk Works'  61, 65, 102
Skyhawk aircraft  97
Skyraider aircraft  82
Smith-Dorrien, General Sir Horace  22
Somme offensive  25
Soviet Naval Air Fleet  88
Sparrow missile  110
Special Survey Flight, RAF  41
Spectrazonal photography  118
Spey turbofan engine  93
'Spikebuoy' acoustic sensor  98
Spitfire aircraft  39–41, 43, 106
'Spooky' gunship aircraft  96
Sputnik 1 satellite  15, 69
'Squat Eye'  97
Standard ARM (Anti-Radiation Missile)  101
Stapf, General  38
'Starlight scope'  83
Sterling radio  26
Steventon, Fl Lt D. W.  42
Stirling aircraft  51
Stratofortress aircraft  74, 99, 100, 103–105
Stratojet aircraft  60
Strike Command, RAF  89
Suez Campaign (1956)  13–15
Sulsi, Commandant  20
Superfortress aircraft  44
Super Sabre aircraft  81
Super Skymaster aircraft  83

T–6 Harvard aircraft  57
T–38 Talon aircraft  104, 105
T1154/R1155 radio  47
TIROS (Television and Infra-Red Observation Satellite)  112
TRAP (Terminal Radiation Airborne measurements Programme)  91
TRE (Telecommunications Research Establishment)  48, 49
Tu–16 (Tupolev 'Badger') aircraft  12, 13, 92
Tu–22 (Tupolev 'Blinder') aircraft  92
Tu–95 (Tupolev 'Bear') aircraft  88, 89
Tu–114 (Tupolev 'Cleat') aircraft  101
Tacco  94
'Tall King'  97
Tactical air co-ordinators  57
Talon aircraft  104, 105

Talos missile  100
Tempelhof Airport (Germany)  33–35
Thor-Able launch vehicle  111, 112
Thornton Pickard Manufacturing Co  25
Thunderchief aircraft  96
Thuy, Xuan  87
Tiger Moth aircraft  108
'Tinsel'  47
Tomcat aircraft  100
'Tree Cat'  97
Trident airliner  103
'Two Spot'  97
Tyuratam (USSR)  113, 119
Type 147 drones  109

U–2 aircraft  61, 64, 66–71, 73, 74, 76, 77, 87, 102, 103
USAF Logistics Command  109
USAF Strategic Air Command  73–75, 100, 103, 104
USAF Tactical Air Command  75
USS *Enterprise*  93
USS *Long Beach*  100
USS *Missouri*  54
United Nations  14, 55, 59
United States Air Force (USAF)  12, 15, 55, 60, 64–66, 74, 76, 91, 96, 97, 103, 109, 110, 114, 115, 122
United States Army Air Force (USAAF)  40, 44, 50, 54
United States Marine Corps (USMC)  58, 96
United States Navy (USN)  55, 58, 74, 76, 90, 96, 97, 118, 123

VFP–62 Squadron, USN  76
VLS (visible light sensor)  117
Vandenburg AFB, California (USA)  15
Vela-type sensor  117, 119
*Vergeltungswaffen* (reprisal weapons)  43–44
Victor aircraft  89, 90, 92
Vidicon TV tube  112
Vigilante aircraft  85, 86, 97
Viking aircraft  93, 118
Visible light sensor (VLS)  117
Voodoo aircraft  76, 78
Vulcan aircraft  89

*War in the Air, The*  23, 25
Wellington aircraft  39, 45, 47, 51
Whitley aircraft  40
'Wild Weasel'  101
'Window'  49–51, 100
Wright Brothers  19

YF–12A aircraft  102

Zeppelin airship  20, 23, 107